DISMANTLING A
Broken
SYSTEM

Actions to Bridge the Opportunity, Equity, and Justice Gap in American Education

ZACHARY WRIGHT

Solution Tree | Press
a division of
Solution Tree

555 North Morton Street
Bloomington, IN 47404
800.733.6786 (toll free) / 812.336.7700
FAX: 812.336.7790

email: info@SolutionTree.com
SolutionTree.com

Printed in the United States of America

Library of Congress Cataloging-in-Publication Data

Names: Wright, Zachary, author.
Title: Dismantling a broken system : actions to bridge the opportunity,
   equity, and justice gap in American education / Zachary Wright.
Description: Bloomington, IN : Solution Tree Press, [2021] | Includes
   bibliographical references and index.
Identifiers: LCCN 2021047292 (print) | LCCN 2021047293 (ebook) | ISBN
   9781952812392 (Paperback) | ISBN 9781952812408 (eBook)
Subjects: LCSH: Educational equalization--United States. | Educational
   change--United States. | Discrimination in education--United States.
Classification: LCC LC4091 .W75 2021 (print) | LCC LC4091 (ebook) | DDC
   379.2/60973--dc23/eng/20211116
LC record available at https://lccn.loc.gov/2021047292
LC ebook record available at https://lccn.loc.gov/2021047293

Solution Tree
Jeffrey C. Jones, CEO
Edmund M. Ackerman, President

Solution Tree Press
President and Publisher: Douglas M. Rife
Associate Publisher: Sarah Payne-Mills
Managing Production Editor: Kendra Slayton
Editorial Director: Todd Brakke
Art Director: Rian Anderson
Copy Chief: Jessi Finn
Senior Production Editor: Tonya Maddox Cupp
Content Development Specialist: Amy Rubenstein
Acquisitions Editor: Sarah Jubar
Copy Editor: Jessi Finn
Proofreader: Evie Madsen
Text and Cover Designer: Laura Cox
Editorial Assistants: Charlotte Jones, Sarah Ludwig, and Elijah Oates

For my students, from whom I have learned so much.

For Laura, always.

Acknowledgments

Huge thanks to the Shoe Crew teachers, leaders, and students who taught me how to teach, in particular Sharif El-Mekki, Kat Schoemaker, David Campbell, Shayna Terrell, Katie Ziemba, Sarah Gentry, and the classes of 2011, 2012, 2013, 2014, 2015, 2016, 2017, 2018, and 2019.

Thanks also to my brightbeam family, who believed in my voice, in particular Ikhlas Saleem, Gordon Wright, Tanesha Peeples, Chioma Oruh, Dirk Tillotson, Nehemiah Frank, Joy Elan, Jason Allen, Maurice Cook, Chris Stewart, and Zakiya Sankara-Jabar.

Shout-out also to my Relay family for believing in me, including Alaina Harper, Aileen Tejeda, TC Carvalho, and Michele Johnsen. Thanks to my first family: my mom, dad, brother, aunts, uncles, and cousins.

Thanks to my UVM family for showing me I could be loved and to my Packer family for the lifelong friendships.

Thanks to my two sons, Leo and Milo, who remind me how to love life and push me to fight for justice every day.

And thanks, finally, to Laura, the love of my life, who saved countless lives and consoled countless families during the COVID-19 pandemic and who pushes me to be a better man, believes in me, and is ever my most steadfast and loving friend.

Solution Tree Press would like to thank the following reviewers:

Molly Capps
Principal
McDeeds Creek Elementary
Southern Pines, North Carolina

Teresa Dobler
Science Teacher
Washington Latin Public Charter School
Washington, D.C.

Jed Kees
Principal
Onalaska Middle School
Onalaska, Wisconsin

Molly Large
Chancellor
Edwin Rhodes Elementary School
Chino, CA

Elizabeth Love
Assistant Principal
Morrison Elementary/Trusty Elementary
Fort Smith, Arkansas

David Ludy
Director of PLC & Instruction
Stanley-Boyd School District
Stanley, WI

Leigh Anne Neal
Assistant Superintendent/Principal
Washington Latin Public Charter School
Washington, D.C.

Amanda Pfeiffer
Assistant Principal
Kealing Middle School
Austin, TX

Jonathan Vander Els
Director of Innovative Projects
New Hampshire Learning Initiative

Trena L. Wilkerson
Professor of Mathematics Education
Baylor University
Waco, TX

Table of Contents

About the Author

Zachary Wright is an assistant professor of practice at Relay Graduate School of Education, serving Philadelphia and Camden, New Jersey, communications activist at brightbeam, curriculum contributor to the Center for Black Educator Development, and general agitator. After beginning his teaching career in early childhood education classrooms, Wright taught eleventh- and twelfth-grade world literature and Advanced Placement literature at Mastery Charter School's Shoemaker Campus, where he served for eight years—including the school's first eight graduating classes.

Wright was a national finalist for the 2018 U.S. Department of Education's School Ambassador Fellowship, and was named Philadelphia's Outstanding Teacher of the Year in 2013. While teaching, Wright created a relationship between Philadelphia's Mastery Schools and the University of Vermont that led to the granting of near-full-ride college scholarships for underrepresented students—a relationship that has seen nearly a dozen college graduates and counting. Wright has also participated in the fight for equitable education funding by testifying before Philadelphia's Board of Education and in the Pennsylvania State Capitol rotunda.

Wright was recruited by Facebook and Edutopia to speak on digital education and in the wake of the COVID-19 pandemic, organized demonstrations to close the digital divide. His writing has been published by *The Philadelphia Inquirer*, *The Philadelphia Citizen*, Chalkbeat, *Educational Leadership*, and numerous education blogs. Wright lives in Collingswood, New Jersey, with his wife and two sons.

Wright earned his bachelor's degree in English from the University of Vermont, his master of English from Villanova University, and his master of education from Cabrini University.

To book Zachary Wright for professional development, contact pd@SolutionTree.com.

Introduction

At 5:30 a.m. on a cold April day in 2012, I found myself sitting at a rectangular classroom table in a dark, otherwise empty high school gymnasium in West Philadelphia, silently looking down at my hands while my seventeen-year-old student, Aisha, and her mother wept. This was my first meeting of the day, the early morning slot to accommodate working families. Aisha (not her real name), her mother, and I had arrived before the building manager would turn the lights on, so we sat together in the ghostly glow of my open laptop.

Aisha was a model student with a strong grade point average, nearly perfect attendance, shining teacher recommendations, and a résumé filled with extracurricular activities and internships that many college graduates would envy. An ambitious young woman with big dreams, ready to become the first member of her family to attend college, she had worked hard, got good grades, served her school community, and navigated a difficult life in one of the poorest zip codes in America's poorest big city, Philadelphia. She had done everything asked of her, and now, here she sat, weeping into the arms of her mother because she could not afford to go to college.

We went over the numbers again. The spreadsheet on my laptop showed the names of the schools to which she had been accepted, nearly a dozen in all, and the total costs of attendance, including tuition, room and board, fees, and miscellaneous expenditures. Deducted from these totals were scholarships, Pell Grants, state grants, and student loan packages, all formulated on her Free Application for Federal Student Aid (FAFSA) that attested to an estimated family contribution of $0. When all was said and done, her cheapest option would cost roughly $10,000 per year out of pocket—an impossibility for her family's income.

I both understood and didn't. I knew Aisha's family and how hard they worked to afford Aisha every possible advantage and how far they stretched the *money they earned. I knew that $10,000 was out of reach. I understood those facts. Nevertheless, there were things I did not understand. I, a White man who had grown up in relative privilege, could not understand the struggle, frustration, and downright injustice of poverty I'd seen here and prior to this in my everyday life. Also, I could not understand how in the United States, the wealthiest country in the history of the planet, a student like Aisha, a role model in nearly every respect, could not achieve her dream of attending a four-year college simply because she did not have enough money. How could that be? How could the system be that broken?*

Aisha's dream school was precisely that—a dream. If Aisha wanted to continue her education, the only option that remained was the local community college, a chronically under-resourced institution with hardworking, well-intentioned staff and a dropout rate of nearly 90 percent. Aisha wiped her eyes and packed up her bag. Supported by her mother, she walked out of the dark gymnasium, the heavy door slamming behind her.

There are experiences in our lives that shape our trajectories and put us on new paths. My morning meeting with Aisha was one such experience.

Perhaps that was a momentous experience because of who I am and because people in the United States get the message that education is the ladder of social mobility—that they can start with nothing or very little and that by going to school, studying, graduating, and working hard, everyone can change the course of their lives, lift themselves out of poverty, and join the American middle (or even upper) class. The message is that education is America's great equalizer and a guarantor against a regimented racial and socioeconomic class system. Americans might tell themselves that education is a public good, a right guaranteed to all regardless of race, class, creed, gender, or religion. There is a clear message that education is the mechanism of the American dream. But as comedian George Carlin and generations of marginalized, disenfranchised Americans have known about the so-called American dream, "you have to be asleep to believe it" (Carlin, Hamza, Mangone, Rickabaugh, & Urbisci, 2005).

That morning in 2012 was when I woke up to the reality that the American education system is a rigged game—rigged against the poor, Black, Latinx, and other marginalized communities, rigged for the benefit of the wealthy, White, and privileged. It is rigged by design by those in power—White men—and by those who continue to benefit from these systems—the wealthy. Rigged by funding formulas and tax structures that empower the wealthy with fully resourced schools and disenfranchise the poor with crumbling educational infrastructures and inexperienced teachers. Rigged by racial, economic, and housing segregation that has created multitiered systems—one for the privileged few, the other for the underprivileged many. Rigged by whitewashed education curricula that omit or distort the truth about the nation's history and ignore the true role people of color have played in the nation's collective history and current events. Rigged by teacher preparatory programs and teacher pipelines that underprepare teachers and underrecruit teachers of color. Rigged by a national apathy to poverty, its inherent trauma, and its impact on children. Rigged, perhaps most of all, by the lies some people tell themselves and the stories they tell their children.

Reformers cannot dismantle America's rigged education system without understanding the racist foundations on which it is built. Though it may seem sweeping to say, nearly every facet of American education can be traced back to the country's roots as a slave-based economy.

- School funding formulas connect to generations of racial segregation.
- Educational inequities such as teacher trainings, placements, and pipelines are traceable to the earliest models of African American education.
- School disciplinary disparities are related to hundreds of years of racial caste systems in America.

This book will go beyond simply naming the inequities by naming specific action steps teachers, school leaders, activists, reformers, and policy makers can take to address and, hopefully, bridge the opportunity, equity, and justice gap in U.S. education.

Why I Wrote This Book

I wrote this book because people can dismantle unjust systems. By the end of this book, I want you to feel inspired to act for change, and I want to arm you with specific action steps to initiate advocacy. In seeing the hugeness of the task before us, resist feeling overwhelmed. Educators can empower themselves with immediate actions to take at the local school level and beyond.

Since my start in education, in 2007, I have been dedicated to learning about and dismantling broken education systems, initially as a classroom teacher serving the first eight graduating classes of Mastery Charter School Shoemaker Campus, a grades 7–12 school in West Philadelphia serving an almost entirely Black community in a zip code whose median income is $21,588 per year (U.S. Census Bureau, 2019). The work started with pushing myself to face the uncomfortable truths of my own privileges, biases, and imperfections, as a non-disabled White male educator who grew up in relative wealth, and the myriad ways I perpetuate the very systems I work to undo.

I struggled, and continue to struggle, with the dissonance and hypocrisy of fighting for an equitable education system while at the same time leveraging the generational wealth and privilege afforded to me by my White family to access quality education for my two sons, a struggle that may feel familiar to some readers. I worked to become a master educator, never ceasing to develop my craft, always assuming the best of my students, and challenging myself to build constant pathways to success for the young people I had the honor to serve. I observed and learned from some of the finest educators in Philadelphia, spoke with and learned from Black students and teachers who grew up in Philadelphia and understood what it means to go to school in the poorest of the country's biggest cities. I pledged to never assume, always ask, and never stop learning.

The work continued as I became a father to a young child of special needs, a brilliant and challenging boy whose passions and intellect are simultaneously gifts and burdens. The work then extended outside my classroom and home to the larger educational landscape as I became more aware of the nature of America's education system and its gross inequities. I delved into the disciplinary data that show wide disparities in school suspensions and expulsions for students of color and students with disabilities, starting first with my local school district. I worked to ensure that adequate mental health supports and social-emotional learning practices were enacted and supported with increased funding on a local ballot initiative. During the COVID-19 pandemic, I worked with activists across the United States lobbying the Federal Communications Commission to ensure that the students without an internet connection at home received access to remote learning. We organized a national day of action against some the nation's largest internet providers. Few things are evidence of a more broken system than millions of children within the richest and most powerful country on Earth being unable to log on to school. I continue the work of highlighting and mitigating educational injustice now as a parent of two young boys, as a teacher educator and coach, and as an education activist.

I am not a clinical psychologist, licensed social worker, historian, professional researcher, principal, or superintendent, nor do I pretend to be any of these things. What I am is an award-winning master educator, teacher leader, activist, and parent of two children. I have taught thousands of students, created curricula, organized demonstrations, documented accelerated student achievement, and advocated for families of children with special needs, including my own.

I did not write this book believing it to be a solution for the injustices rooted in our country; rather, I wrote this book to ensure K–12 teachers and administrators have a solid, research-based understanding of the systemic oppression riddling U.S. education and know actions to advocate for and create equity inside and outside their own schools, all the while understanding that each chapter's focus could fill volumes in its own right. This book simply contains the truths I have seen in education since my start in 2007 and truths that come from others' research—truths that I believe can compel anyone who professes a commitment to justice to stand up and speak out.

There will be points in this book when I come off as angry. In some sections, I may sound impassioned or accusing. Indeed, I've been told at times to tamp down the ferocity with which I write. But there is a reason behind the tone. There is sadness in this book. A lot in this book can make action seem impossible, even for those like me, who have not personally endured racism. The anger serves to counteract the sedating nature of sadness. This book's tone is sometimes angry for the precise reason that the injustices described are infuriating. It is my hope that any anger you also feel, combined with the actions and examples this book provides, will serve as a spark that will light the fire of activism. As Malcolm X (1965b) once said, "Usually when people are sad, they don't do anything. They just cry over their condition. But when they get angry, they bring about a change."

Who This Book Is For and How This Book Is Organized

This book is for any educator interested in pondering how U.S. education works and how it is rigged against marginalized communities. This brief book will allow readers to consider many areas of bias and roadblocks that are built into U.S. education against marginalized communities, and, in this way, individually and as teams ponder opportunity, equity, and justice gaps in their classrooms, schools, and communities and contemplate how to become activists for doable improvement at a local level. It will empower principals and district leaders with activities and exercises to recruit, develop, and lead anti-racist staff. This book will also empower activists with data, research, and action steps to agitate for justice in their own communities. Through all of these actions, the hope is that this book will help break down the broken system that so unjustly failed Aisha, her family, and so many others.

This book is organized into four chapters aligned with injustices that have created and perpetuated a broken U.S. education system.

Chapter 1 delves into America's history of slavery and racism and its clear impacts on education policy going back all the way to 1619 and continuing in classrooms of the 21st century. The chapter also includes ways for educators and school leaders to mitigate the negative impacts of racism and implicit biases in their schools. Chapter 2 tackles the labyrinth that makes up educational funding in America, including funding formulas, taxation, and the resulting commoditization of so-called public education and also provides funding policy proposals. Chapter 3 deals with broken systems of American teacher training and preparatory programs by naming specific ways to incentivize and train the next generation of teachers in an effort to ensure that all students have outstanding teachers. Finally, chapter 4 discusses the unproductive and unnecessary turf wars between educational camps such as unions, charter schools, and educational reformers and the ways such disagreements undercut the students for whom all groups supposedly advocate.

Each chapter includes the following elements.

- An explanation of how the American education system serves to create the rigged game of education

- Action steps specified for teachers and school leaders in the How to Make Change sections

- Lighthouse Beacons, which spotlight educators and activists who, through their tireless work, point the way toward educational justice and equity

- Reflection Questions, which readers answer as individuals and teams to ponder how they can become change makers in their own communities

Before we continue, let me tell you a story. One day early in my teaching career, my building principal asked me the following question: "What would you have done if you were around during the civil rights movement?" My mind filled with images of freedom rides, sit-ins, marches, and demonstrations. I told myself I would have done it all! Next, the principal said, "Well, whatever you would have done, you better start now, because the civil rights movement is happening now" (S. El Mekki, personal communication, August 2021). So long as the education system denies students their right to quality education, the work of dismantling broken systems and bridging the opportunity, equity, and justice gaps in American education continues. So long as schools are funded by zip code, so long as students of color face a school-to-prison pipeline, and so long as the least prepared and least experienced teachers are funneled into under-resourced schools, the work continues. The road is long, but we will walk it together.

Let's get to work.

America's History of Racism, Color Blindness, and Implicit Bias

To dismantle a broken system, we must first understand the rotten foundations on which the system is built. We must understand the intentions, impacts, designs, and methods of an unjust system if we aim to create a more equitable system. This chapter's purpose is to help establish this necessary level of understanding. Only by understanding America's start and its enslaved economy, quasi-education, *Brown v. Board of Education of Topeka* (1954) as a complicated victory, so-called color blindness, and school discipline can teachers, administrators, reformers, activists, and policy makers begin to dismantle America's broken education system.

America's Start and Its Enslaved Economy

America's growing economic might rested on the shoulders of enslaved people. While there may be some debate as to whether 1619 marks the true starting point of slavery in America (Waxman, 2019), the fact remains that America's rapid ascent onto the world stage would not have been possible without the kidnapping, forced enslavement, and violent exploitation of Africans by European colonists. As Pulitzer Prize–winning reporter Nikole Hannah-Jones (2019) explains, "It was the relentless buying, selling, insuring and financing of [enslaved] bodies and the products of their labor that made Wall Street a thriving banking, insurance and trading sector and New York City the financial capital of the world." This is not hyperbole. Numbers lay out the truth behind the words: "At the height of slavery [cotton] was the nation's most valuable commodity, accounting for half of all American exports and 66 percent of the world's supply" (Hannah-Jones, 2019). Just like the South's, the North's industrial and financial might was also built with stolen human beings and forced labor.

The entire U.S. economy was built on a system that would suffer if enslaved people received access to education. In *1845*, escaped slave and American social reformer, abolitionist, and statesman Frederick Douglass (1845/2002) illustrates this power of education. Enslaved, Douglass was taught to read and write by someone he refers to as Mistress Hughes, who quickly stopped teaching Douglass for fear his learning would be incompatible with his enslavement (Douglass, 1845/2002). He describes the momentous impact that learning to read had on his understanding of his situation:

> [Reading] had given me a view of my wretched condition, without the remedy. It opened my eyes to the horrible pit, but to no ladder upon which to get out. In moments of agony, I envied my fellow-slaves for their stupidity. I have often wished myself a beast. I preferred the condition of the meanest reptile to my own. Any thing, no matter what, to get rid of thinking! It was this everlasting thinking of my condition that tormented me. There was no getting rid of it . . . Freedom now appeared, to disappear no more forever. It was heard in every sound, and seen in every thing. (Douglass, 1845/2002, p. 58)

Frederick Douglass's firsthand account clearly presents both the vehemence with which education was restricted and the incalculable impact of education on enslaved people. Free, widespread, and accessible education was something enslavers passionately opposed because they wanted to continue a slave economy; education would open a window onto the world beyond slavery. Accordingly, both law and custom strictly prohibited educating people who were free and enslaved:

> That all meetings or assemblages of slaves, or free negroes or mulattoes mixing and associating with such slaves at any meeting-house or houses, &c., in the night; or at any SCHOOL OR SCHOOLS for teaching them READING OR WRITING, either in the day or night, under whatsoever pretext, shall be deemed and considered an UNLAWFUL ASSEMBLY (Goodell, 1853, pp. 319–320)

In this way, outlawing a Black person's right to an education was not just about reading and writing, but about outlawing the existence of a community outside of White jurisdiction. Education, in its outlawing, was a means of protecting and consolidating White power. Then, as now, the fight for access to education goes beyond the classroom; it is about liberation and the actualization of one's full humanity.

Slavery, bigotry, ubiquitous racial inequality, and White supremacy did not end after the Civil War but adapted and morphed. As legal scholar and civil rights lawyer Michelle Alexander (2020) tells it, "This deep faith in white supremacy not only justified an economic and political system in which plantation owners acquired land and great wealth . . . it also endured . . . long after the historical circumstances that gave rise to [it] passed away" (p. 27). The deep foundations of human bondage set the stage for what would come next: decisions about who to educate, how, and why, that led to the establishment of a rigged system of education whose dismantling is long overdue.

Quasi-Education

Education is inherently political. Educating someone—or refusing to educate someone—is political. What to educate someone about is political. Even the choice not to discuss politics in schools is a political act, one that "bolsters the status quo" (Walker, 2018). The decisions of who to educate, how, and why reflect the political agenda and mores of the economically and politically powerful.

Following the Civil War, the Northern industrialists' growing might and their political and economic self-interest dominated the developing nation's economic landscape. A war-torn nation on the brink of mass industrialization required stability and a steady supply of laborers. The industrialists guided education policy and felt newly emancipated people fit the bill of education policy in America.

Perhaps no figure played a more critical, influential role in the creation and trajectory of education for Black Americans after the Civil War than Samuel Chapman Armstrong (National Park Service, 2015). Armstrong developed a model of education, which came to be known as the *Hampton model*, which served to fill the needs of postwar America, providing racial and social stability while at the same time creating a labor force educated about agriculture and industry (National Park Service, 2015). The goal of this education is evidenced by not only *what* students were taught—"helpful work"— but also what was *denied* to them—"higher mathematics" (Watkins, 2001, p. 50).

Industrialists in the North and powerful White people across the South desired peaceable Black Americans content with a partial education and partial freedom. Thus, the Hampton model "became the model for the ideological training for the Black South" (Watkins, 2001, p. 61). Eager to perpetuate this form of education, North industrialists started pouring their dollars into schools; the Rockefellers, for example, donated millions (Goldberg & Shubinski, 2020). It would take until midway through the 20th century for Black people to gain further education rights—this time in Topeka, Kansas.

Brown v. Board of Education—A Complicated Victory

Brown v. Board of Education, which determined that racially segregated education was unconstitutional, was the "defining moment" that discredited the "legal rationale underpinning the racial caste system that had been endorsed or accepted by governments at all levels since the end of the nineteenth century" (NAACP Legal Defense and Educational Fund, n.d.).

The *Brown* decision also eventually destroyed the Black teaching profession. Between 1954 and 1965, thirty-eight thousand Black American teachers and principals lost their jobs (Lutz, 2017). By some estimates, 93 percent of the Black teaching force was displaced (Peters, 2019). While this story is almost never told, its inevitability is not altogether surprising. For one, the Supreme Court's attempt at desegregation was a one-way street because "desegregation closed Black schools, not White ones, and displaced Black educators, not White ones" (Peters, 2019, p. 531). Since Black schools closed and Black students were sent into White schools, Black teachers were fired—in some cases, rehired by administrators at White schools—who might have fought against desegregation in the first place. It is no surprise, then, that the Black teaching profession was essentially gutted.

The impact of the destruction of the Black teaching profession is still felt. Only "11% of public school principals are Black, while over 50% of students in schools are people of color" (Peters, 2019, p. 524). For teachers, the rates are even more alarming. Black teachers make up less than 10 percent of the American teacher workforce, even though more than half of students identify as people of color (National Center for Education Statistics [NCES], 2021b). The lack of teachers of color in American schools hurts all students. According to Desiree Carver-Thomas of the Learning Policy Institute (2018):

> The benefit [to Black students] of having a Black teacher for just 1 year in elementary school can persist over several years [and] students of color and White students also report having positive perceptions of their teachers of color, including feeling cared for and academically challenged. (pp. v, 4)

The lack of teachers of color in American schools is a self-perpetuating problem. After all, with so few students of color seeing teachers who are not White, it is unsurprising that these students do not choose to become teachers themselves.

In addition to nearly eradicating the Black teaching population, the Supreme Court framed its *Brown* decision in a way that implied Blackness was a barrier to learning, enshrining proximity to Whiteness as the cure-all for educational injustice. Rather than identifying White racism as the cause of educational injustice, the court argued that what Black students truly needed was to have White classmates (Lutz, 2017). The court did not discuss the resource inequity that caused inequities in Black education and White education but simply moved Black individuals into White spaces. These beliefs became further entrenched in the early 1970s when U.S. President Richard Nixon refused to increase funds for Black schools, saying, "No, they don't need money; they don't need newer books; they don't need new facilities; they don't need infrastructure. What they need is to sit next to little White children" (as cited in Milner & Howard, 2004, p. 292).

It is worth pausing for a moment to imagine a scenario that became all too common: Black students, their former schools closed and their teachers fired, redistributed into majority-White schools, taught by teachers who did not look like them and who may have been against desegregation in the first place. No longer able to segregate between schools, schools began to segregate *in* schools, creating separate tracks of learning: "Black students were labeled and tracked into the lowest academic areas, and . . . all of a sudden the White students magically turned into gifted children" (Milner & Howard, 2004, p. 293). For example, studies show that by middle school, "Hispanic and black students were most likely to enroll in the standard math course and less likely than average to take one of the three advanced courses typically taken by white students" (Sparks, 2020). In fact, in states like North Carolina, in-school segregation accounted for nearly half of all racial segregation in public schools (Sparks, 2020).

Schools largely continue this legacy. New York City's famous and widely respected Stuyvesant High School has somehow admitted fewer than fifteen Black students a year out of thousands of applicants from all demographics (Shapiro, 2021). Similarly, Philadelphia's Masterman School, another magnet school in a majority-non-White city, is a majority-White school. These realities descend directly from slavery, the Hampton model, Jim Crow, and *Brown v. Board of Education*, and the continued commodification of American education.

In spite of these facts, most American schools laud *Brown v. Board of Education of Topeka* (1954) every February alongside Martin Luther King Jr. and Rosa Parks but do not acknowledge the absence of Black educators. Why is that? Why do American curricula teach slavery as an unfortunate chapter of the past that is over rather than the building block on which America stands? Why do conversations about education and justice so rarely acknowledge the White supremacist roots and continuations within U.S. education and focus instead on grit and a so-called *achievement gap*? The answer is because that is part of how the game is rigged. The maintenance of White supremacy needs a guilt-free, color-blind lens through which to see the world. It requires deflecting the inquisitive gaze of history from the self in the present to others in the past.

Color Blindness and School Discipline

America's commitment to color blindness creates the illusion of progress by allowing someone to say things like "I don't see color," or, "I don't care if he's Black, Brown, or purple," and free oneself of the burden of facing racism (Alexander, 2020). America's commitment to color blindness has effectively, subtly, and insidiously maintained racial inequities from housing, to incarceration, health, and of course, education. Every year, sometime during Black History Month, students around the country learn about the beauty and impassioned pleas of tolerance found in Martin Luther King's (1963/2010) "I Have a Dream" speech. It is held up as the ultimate expression of Americaness, a commitment to racial idealism in which all are treated equally. But White America has used one line of the speech—"I have a dream that my four little children will one day live in a nation where they will not be judged by the color of their skin but by the content of their character" (King, 1963/2010)—to codify color blindness as the true goal of racial understanding. It is a somewhat ironic twist that the man who was once called "the most dangerous Negro of the future in this Nation from the standpoint of communism, the Negro and national security'" has now in many ways been transformed into a hero of color blindness (APM Reports, n.d.).

The truth is that color blindness has been, in Michelle Alexander's (2020) word, *catastrophic*. Race-neutral language has provided the cover needed to enact racist policies while claiming that since the policies are color blind, racism cannot be a factor in any resulting inequity. Although explicitly racial language is not used to describe drug criminals, the heavy use of images of Black men during the country's war on drugs makes it explicitly clear what the country's enemy in that so-called war looks like (Jarecki & Shopsin, 2012).

Color blindness creates the narrative that rules are all race neutral and punishment for rule breaking is solely based on people's individual failings. Color blindness, in short, "prevents us from seeing the racial and structural divisions that persist in society: the segregated, unequal schools, the segregated, jobless ghettos" (Alexander, 2020, p. 241). This color blindness has had disastrous impacts in schools across the country, particularly in the implementation of disciplinary practices.

During the Obama administration, the Department of Education encouraged school districts across the country to investigate their disciplinary practices and identify any possible civil rights abuses. The data from 2014 (figure 1.1) demonstrate the wide disparities in school discipline between White students and students of color.

Consider the following disparities:

- Black children represent 18% of preschool enrollment, but 48% of preschool children receiving more than one out-of-school suspension. In comparison, white students represent 43% of preschool enrollment but 26% of preschool children receiving more than one out-of-school suspension.

- Black students are suspended and expelled at a rate three times greater than white students. On average, 5% of white students are suspended, compared to 16% of black students.

- Black girls are suspended at higher rates (12%) than girls of any other race or ethnicity.

- While black students represent 16% of student enrollment, they represent 27% of students referred to law enforcement and 31% of students subjected to a school-related arrest. In comparison, white students represent 51% of enrollment, 41% of students referred to law enforcement, and 39% of those arrested. (U.S. Department of Education Office for Civil Rights, 2014, p. 1)

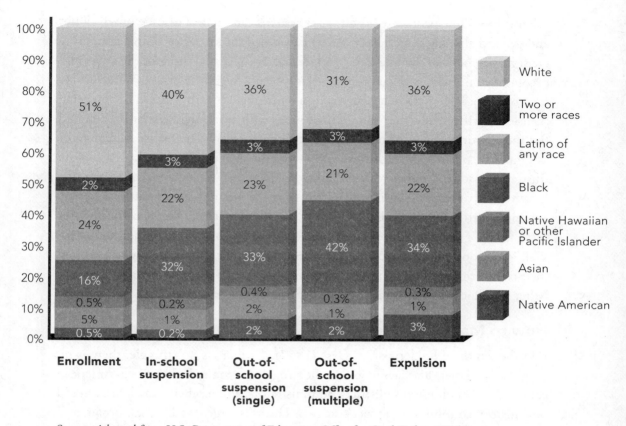

Source: Adapted from U.S. Department of Education Office for Civil Rights, 2014.

Figure 1.1: Students receiving suspensions and expulsions, by race and ethnicity.

These disciplinary disparities are all results of a race-neutral, color-blind, and profoundly racist system of education. Yet, when faced with these numbers, a common White response is one not of impassioned activism but of skepticism: "What did these students do? What do the teachers have to say? Do these students come from two-parent households? Maybe these students just don't know how to behave." These responses expose a latent racism that assumes the worst about Black and Brown children, which is a racism that seeps into all facets of schooling and education and contributes to those students' chronic absenteeism, increased drop-out rates, and greater likelihood of incarceration (NCES, 2021b).

These responses, as widespread as they are infuriating, are expressions of what has come to be known as *White fragility*, an emotional response White people can have when confronted with their perhaps unintentionally racist acts or viewpoints (DiAngelo, 2018). The questions about the data are, in truth, questions about whether racism exists in the first place.

For some White people, to admit racist systems can invite a cascade of self-doubt and ground-shaking uncertainty. Being called out for saying or doing something racist makes many of them respond with denial. Some may try to turn the tables and become the ones who need comforting. This is White fragility in action. White people can combat a knee-jerk defensive reaction by taking a breath. Instead of emptying their lungs with words, they can fill their lungs with a calming breath. They should feel the emotions raised by inadvertently making a racially insensitive statement or assumption coursing through their body—the possible embarrassment, confusion, frustration, sadness, and anger. And if they do defensively react with words, after the breath, they can say something like, "I'm sorry. It was not my intent to say or do anything hurtful. However, I acknowledge that my intent does not take priority over my impact. If you are willing to explain what I did wrong, I am willing to listen." Well-intentioned people, including educators, make mistakes, but they needn't lose their commitment to learning and doing better. The bottom line is that it is always better to acknowledge and face one's biases in order to learn and grow and change.

How to Make Change

In the words of Frederick Douglass (1857), "If there is no struggle, there is no progress," and there are ways to join in the struggle for equity and justice in American education. School systems, districts, administrators, and teachers can all understand how history continues to impact students. Districts large, small, rural, urban, and suburban can mine vast collections of data, free and publicly available, to identify disparities in discipline and educational opportunity. Teachers can include and highlight new and classic works by non-White people in school curricula, and White people, both in and out of education, can be guided, supported, and challenged to do difficult introspective work that is not only necessary to mitigate the impact of implicit biases on students and families, but is also necessary modeling for other White parents doing their own introspection. This work is difficult, but it can be done in every classroom.

The following sections cover some ideas for how to make progress in classrooms and districts to address systemic inequities and racial injustices.

- Teach history with culturally diverse texts.
- Train culturally responsive teachers.
- Go beyond heroes and holidays.
- Read and discuss equity literacy case studies.
- Participate in the privilege-for-sale activity.
- Develop hyperlocal activism with community-run equity committees.
- Ensure all schools have a solid tiered support system.

Teach History With Culturally Diverse Texts

As a part of culturally responsive teaching, curricula and texts given to students must challenge the false notions of color blindness and post-racial harmony. Examples of texts that critically challenge America's conception of race are as follows.

- *Just Mercy: A Story of Justice and Redemption* by Bryan Stevenson (2019)

- *Bury My Heart at Wounded Knee* by Dee Brown (1970)

- *Killing the White Man's Indian: Reinventing of Native Americans at the End of the Twentieth Century* by Fergus M. Bordewich (1996)

- *The New Jim Crow: Mass Incarceration in the Age of Colorblindness* by Michelle Alexander (2020)

- *The Autobiography of Malcolm X* as told to Alex Haley (1965a)

- *The Warmth of Other Suns: The Epic Story of America's Great Migration* by Isabel Wilkerson (2010)

- The works of Toni Morrison, specifically *Beloved* (Morrison, 1987)

- *Killing Rage: Ending Racism* by bell hooks (1995)

- *Other People's Children: Cultural Conflict in the Classroom* by Lisa Delpit (2006)

- *The BreakBeat Poets: New American Poetry in the Age of Hip-Hop* edited by Kevin Coval, Quraysh Ali Lansana, and Nate Marshall (2015)

- *The Color of Law: A Forgotten History of How Our Government Segregated America* by Richard Rothstein (2017)

- *The Lost Education of Horace Tate: Uncovering the Hidden Heroes Who Fought for Justice in Schools* by Vanessa Siddle Walker (2018)

- The works of W. E. B. Du Bois, James Baldwin, Richard Wright, and Ralph Ellison

Crucial historical figures are as follows.

- **Paul Beatty:** A master satirist, Beatty's fiction, in particular his novel *The Sellout* (Beatty, 2015), illuminates the tragic absurdity of racism in America.

- **Zora Neale Hurston:** Unapologetically authentic in her use of vernacular and commitment to storytelling, Hurston is a must read for all.

- **Ann Petry:** Overshadowed by the likes of Richard Wright, Petry's (1946) novel *The Street* is a heartbreaking rendering of the impact of systemic racism on a young mother and her son.

- **Colson Whitehead:** An imaginative and fearless storyteller, Whitehead's many novels weave analysis of race and culture effortlessly, unafraid to challenge traditions, most evidenced in his award-winning *The Underground Railroad* (Whitehead, 2016).

Concepts and sources that expand, complicate, and deepen an understanding of America's history of injustice are as follows.

- The Equal Justice Initiative (https://eji.org), founded by Bryan Stevenson, which tells the history of American violence against black bodies
- America's legacy of lynching Black people, from Emmett Till to Kalief Browder, in books including *Beyond the Rope: The Impact of Lynching on Black Culture and Memory* (Hill, 2016) and *At the Hands of Persons Unknown: The Lynching of Black America* (Dray, 2003)
- The 1619 Project (https://nyti.ms/3EeBuCJ; Hannah-Jones, 2019)
- Voices of the Latinx community, including Juan González and the Chicano Movement
- Voices of the Asian community, including Asian Americans Advancing Justice (www.advancingjustice-aajc.org)
- Voices of Japanese and Japanese Americans regarding internment during World War II, such as *Farewell to Manzanar* by Jeanne Wakatsuki Houston and James D. Houston (1973)
- Voices of those in the LGBTQ communities, including those during the Stonewall riots as well as the Human Rights Campaign (www.hrc.org)
- For elementary school-level resources, please see Colorful Stories (https://colorfulstories.org)

While it may be true that some of this material is not appropriate for the youngest elementary students, consider speaking about topics in an age-appropriate manner. If you want to avoid a topic or resource, consider whether it is developmentally inappropriate for the student's age, or whether you fear it might simply make students uncomfortable. If a resource is truly developmentally inappropriate, then do not use it. However, fear of making students uncomfortable is not a reason to avoid a particular topic or resource. Research proves, in fact, that students of all races benefit from such conversations (Cabrera, Milem, Jaquette, & Marx, 2014; Dee & Penner, 2016, 2019)

Train Culturally Responsive Teachers

Teacher training programs, districts, and schools should prepare, coach, and continuously support their teachers in becoming culturally responsive anti-racist educators who support anti-racist policies through their actions or expressions (Kendi, 2019). Not doing so, or assuming that culturally responsive professional development is somebody else's responsibility, is to show willful ignorance about the needs of students across the country.

What does it mean to be a culturally responsive teacher? Succinctly put, it means to infuse teaching practices with a thorough and continuously developing cultural consciousness (Hammond, 2015) and the "awareness that one's worldview is not universal but is profoundly shaped by one's life experiences" (Villegas & Lucas, 2002, p. 27). One's point of view is precisely that—one point of view. The existence and experience of a Latinx person from a city are likely quite different from those of a White person from the suburbs, which are different from those of a Native American person living on a ranch, which are different from those of a Black person living in rural America, and so on. These differences exist without moral judgment. One's cultural expression is not inferior or superior to another's. These differences exist, and they ought to be recognized and honored.

Understanding the nation's changing demographics makes the need for culturally responsive educators all the clearer. By the dawn of the 21st century, more than one out of every three students enrolled in public elementary and secondary schools were of a racial or ethnic minority (NCES, 2021b). Since then, that number has only risen. The diversity of the teaching workforce, however, has not kept pace with the demographic shifts of students. Not even close. While children of color represent upwards of 35 percent of the national student population, teachers of color make up less than 10 percent (NCES, 2021b). For true culturally responsive teaching to happen in schools across America, it is imperative that more classrooms be led by Black and Latinx teachers.

Considering the rigid and deeply entrenched segregation systems described in this book, and the pervasive opportunity gap between students in predominantly White schools and students in predominantly non-White schools (discussed in chapter 2, page 29), the negative impact of a student of color never having a teacher of color cannot be overstated. As teacher educator Zaretta Hammond (2015) demonstrates in her work:

> Underserved English learners, poor students, and students of color routinely receive less instruction in higher order skills development than other students. . . . This type of instruction denies students the opportunity to engage in what neuroscientists call *productive struggle* that actually grows [their] brainpower. (pp. 12–13)

In short, underserved students are taught below-grade-level materials with an emphasis on test taking rather than higher-order-thinking skills like comparative analysis and critical thinking—skills increasingly necessary. This gap is often due to the implicit biases teachers have about students, particular across lines of difference (Education Trust, 2020). A more diverse teaching pool can help mitigate these biased expectations of students and ensure that all students engage in rigorous instruction.

While this, of course, does not mean that White teachers cannot or should not teach non-White students, it does mean that all teachers—White and non-White—need specific training, coaching, and support in ensuring their teaching practices empower students, rather than oppress them.

To be culturally conscious and culturally responsive is, at the same time, to understand that race does not equal sameness. Simply because two people share a race does not mean they share a love of certain music, food, books, or clothing. It is this fallacy that sees many novice teachers assuming that they should teach a classroom full of Black students a lesson using rap, or that a classroom full of Latinx students must love reggaeton or soccer. Students are people, and while people share cultures, they also embody individualized expressions and tastes. The culturally responsive teacher is constantly aware of all these things.

The following exercise can help illuminate someone who is not currently culturally responsive by helping participants who have not already developed their identity lenses—their ability to see realities and potential injustices beyond their own experiences. Staff should engage in this three-step exercise before a school year begins. As teachers return from break and school leaders begin to prepare for the school year, all teachers and administrators should come together for an activity. Once all teachers are assembled, school leaders distribute three index cards to each teacher and do the following to have the teachers take part in the three steps.

1. Show teachers a list of (necessarily incomplete) common identity markers: gender, race, class, ability, language, body type, gender expression, religion, and age. Teachers write each marker on a separate index card and rank the identity markers in order of importance based on *how they see themselves*. For some, religion is a powerful part of their identity and therefore ranks toward the top of the list, while people often overlook ability and place it toward the bottom. When everyone has finished ranking, teachers record how they ranked the markers.

2. Have teachers shuffle their identity marker cards and re-rank them based on *how other people see them*. The rankings this time likely look different. While a person may not see social markers such as race or gender identity as being particularly important to identity, it is often highly important for others. Teachers begin to see how the power of identity markers varies based on viewpoint.

3. Have teachers now imagine their future students and rank identity markers about themselves based on *how they think their students will see them*. Teachers record their rankings, revisit them a month into the school year, and reflect on their findings. For many, their predictions will end up being wildly inaccurate, providing fodder for thoughtful reflection at a later

date, when all teachers are brought together once again to revisit their assumptions a few months into the school year.

Once the school year begins, it is imperative that teachers and administrators continue their professional learning toward becoming culturally responsive educators. Forming collaborative teams—"communities within schools, composed of voluntary participating teachers with a specific task to accomplish" (Schaap & de Bruijn, 2018, p. 109)—is a valuable way to continue this work. In this case, the teams' task is fostering teacher cultural competency.

These collaborative teams' conversations can be challenging, but when done well, they can truly change a school's culture. Some ways to maximize the chances of collaborative team success are creating norms, prioritizing process over product, garnering feedback, and ensuring that teams include school leaders but are led by teachers.

Each team should create and decide on norms, but those should include at least some of the following.

- **This is a brave space, rather than a safe space:** This is a team meeting space where we speak our truths, push one another to explain our points of view, and push one another to consider alternative perspectives.

- **We are comfortable with discomfort:** When conversations get uncomfortable (but not hostile), that is a sign that we are doing necessary work; we lean into discomfort and understand that the work will not end, nor will problems be solved, when the meeting is over.

- **We prioritize impact over intention:** If someone says something that hurts someone, the speaker receives the feedback and apologizes, and the conversation moves on. We do not prioritize the speaker's intent over the speaker's impact on the team.

Creating and revisiting these norms is essential to build the trust and buy-in necessary to engage in the conversations that will take place. With these norms established and referred to, collaborative teams have a strong foundation to tackle what matters most—students—which is precisely where conversations should begin.

Collaborative team discussions are most effective when based on tangible school experiences. The following are good places to start.

- School disciplinary data

- Student write-ups with student names redacted

- Case studies on diversity (page 21)

The most successful teams avoid pushing participants toward a "correct" answer. Implying a correct answer is the best way to lose trust. Instead, team leaders should prioritize conversation, debate, and valuing of differing truths.

Go Beyond Heroes and Holidays

In a training on culturally responsive teaching, I was introduced to a theory called the *stages of multicultural curriculum transformation* (Gorski, n.d.). Two of its stages are described here.

1. **Curriculum of the mainstream:** Default curricula, otherwise known as *curricula of the mainstream*, are Eurocentric and male centric. For example, default curricula often involve teaching students about Christopher Columbus without mentioning Native American genocide; never teaching students about Egypt except when discussing pyramids and mummies; teaching *Adventures of Huckleberry Finn* (Twain, 1884) but not *Beloved* (Morrison, 1987); or analyzing the Declaration of Independence with students without also reading the Declaration of the Rights of Woman and of the Female Citizen.

2. **Heroes and holidays:** Many schools find themselves here. This is when teachers "'celebrate' difference by integrating information or resources about famous people and the cultural artifacts of various groups into the mainstream curriculum," creating bulletin boards with significant people and focusing on traditions such as food and music (Gorski, n.d.).

Stage 2 may sound positive. It sounds like students are learning to honor other cultures, value tolerance, appreciate diversity, and be kind to all. But there are several problems here. Celebrating Black History Month, LGBTQ Pride Month, or Women's History Month makes it so these nondominant groups are *othered*—outside the norm (Osborn, 2018). They exist outside the context of the real curriculum; they are the intermissions between the "real" work. Therefore, when that month concludes, it is akin to the teacher saying, "Now, let's get back to our regularly scheduled programming." In addition, focusing solely on larger-than-life figures gives students the message that these heroes represent the entirety of the nondominant experience. It doesn't allow students to fully grasp the inequitable conditions that people of nondominant groups face. This is important because this practice perpetuates the theory of Black exceptionalism. Paraphrasing Michelle Alexander (2020), *Black exceptionalism* is the belief that since there are some Black people who have succeeded, then the system must, in fact, be equitable and accessible for all. As Alexander (2020) notes:

> Black success stories lend credence to the notion that anyone, no matter how poor or how black you may be, can make it to the top, if only you try hard enough. These stories "prove" that race is no longer relevant. (p. 248)

Getting beyond heroes and holidays requires going beyond the anecdotal mentioning of nondominant groups. It is crucial to integrate these voices into the everyday curriculum.

Read and Discuss Equity Literacy Case Studies

To build on the activity about identity markers, teachers should develop *equity literacy*—the ability to see, understand, and mitigate injustice (Gorski & Pothini, 2018). As described earlier, the post–civil rights era, with its race-neutral language, has strengthened the myth that sufferings of wide swaths of the U.S. population are due not to systemic injustice but to personality flaws. Belief in a so-called culture of poverty blames those living in poverty for their plight, rather than the inequitable education, housing, health, and criminal justice systems that create vast webs of injustice. It is simply impossible for a teacher with such a deficit mindset to adequately serve students, for "no set of curricular or pedagogical strategies can turn a classroom led by a teacher with a deficit view of families experiencing poverty into an equitable learning space for those families" (Gorski, 2016, p. 381). For teachers to equitably serve their students as culturally responsive educators, they need to be able to see these systems of injustice, rather than blame students and their families for demonstrating symptoms of poverty. Developing their equity literacy helps them do precisely that. Teachers who work to develop their equity literacy skills become "a threat to the existence of bias and inequity" in their classrooms (Gorski & Pothini, 2018, p. 10).

Case studies provide fantastic opportunities for teachers to develop their equity literacy and their cultural responsiveness. Gorski and Pothini's (2018) *Case Studies on Diversity and Social Justice Education* presents teachers with short scenarios familiar to all teachers: parent-teacher conferences, school dances, homework policies, special education services, students learning English as a second language, Black History Month, school discipline, and so forth. Teachers read the scenario and engage in a systematic process by which they do the following in small groups or teams.

1. Understand what is happening in the scenario.
2. Take stock of all points of view by naming all the parties involved, as well as their intentions and impacts.
3. Identify potential injustices.
4. Imagine what justice would look like.
5. Brainstorm short- and long-term solutions.

These case studies, combined with the identity marker exercise, help teachers see the world outside their own perspective, identify systemic injustice, and sharpen their change-agent skills.

Participate in the Privilege-for-Sale Activity

The ideals of individualism, raising oneself by the bootstraps, fairness, and meritocracy are White American. Individualism, similar to color blindness, erases America's history of racial injustice by ignoring systemic racism and focusing only on the self. To believe in hard work and individualism is to believe that the fruits of people's labor are entirely due to their own efforts, not attributable at all to a system that has been designed for them. To believe in bootstraps relieves one from wondering why it is that entire communities struggle. If one can succeed through hard work, then surely everyone should be able to. For educators to become truly culturally responsive, they must dive into the work of analyzing privilege.

In an exercise known as *privilege for sale* (Bolger, n.d.), teachers and school leaders can reflect on the immense impact having, or not having, different privileges can have on one's life. In the privilege-for-sale exercise, participants, such as teachers or students, are placed in small groups of between three and five people. Each group is told that it lacks any and all societal privileges. Each group receives a predetermined amount of play money in different denominations: $100, $300, $500, $700, and $1,000. After each group has its own money, each gets a privilege menu—a list of various societal privileges, each costing $200. Examples of these privileges include, but are not limited to, the following.

- Access to health care

- Access to transportation

- Access to new clothing

- The ability to keep my home a comfortable temperature

- Access to a grocery store with healthy food options

- Access to reliable housing

- Access to college regardless of cost

- The expectation that I will have a day off from work or school for a holiday I observe

- The expectation that people will pronounce my name correctly

- The expectation that police are there to protect me and my family

- The expectation that people of races different from my own will not remind me of my race

- The ability to see myself in the books I read, classes I take, and teachers who teach me

- The expectation that when I enter a store, a security guard will not follow me

- The ability to be seen as an individual rather than a member of a race or group

- The ability to not be reminded of my race
- The ability to present a Social Security number
- The right to vote
- The ability to not worry about citizenship status
- The ability to use the bathroom that matches my gender identity
- The right to marry whomever I choose
- The ability to identify my gender identity on forms
- The ability to walk comfortably in my neighborhood after dark
- The ability to walk up stairs
- The ability to speak English

The groups then have about ten minutes during which to spend their money to purchase their societal privileges. Once the exercise is over, the reflection work begins. Participants come together in their small groups to discuss the following questions (Bolger, n.d.).

- What was doing this activity like?
- What questions or struggles did the group tackle when deciding which privileges to buy?
- What trends did you notice in terms of which privileges were valued and why?
- Did your group members tend to agree or disagree on which privileges to purchase? What could this mean?
- What will you take away from the experience of completing this activity?

The privilege-for-sale exercise presents an intriguing, safe, and equitable way of engaging with societal privilege and reflecting on the privileges participants may or may not enjoy or perhaps have never recognized.

 Personal Interlude: *I Can't Spare My Son His Struggles, But I Can Be There When He Triumphs*

I had to drag my son kicking and screaming into kindergarten. His anxiety had taken over, and his mind was spinning. Kindergarten was too fast. Recess was too short. The cafeteria was too loud. And my heart broke.

What nobody told me, but what every parent knows, is that aiding one's children through childhood brings us back to our own childhood years. Seeing my son struggle, painful as it was, was even more so because it reminded me of own struggles with anxiety, depression, and panic. Trying to soothe my boy, I was transported back decades. There I was, a terrified boy, probably ten or so, hiding in bathrooms, trying to breathe, convinced of my own eventual insanity. There I was, a quiet boy trying to avoid the notice of the older kids; refusing to get out of the car to go into day camp; paralyzed with fear at being called on to present in front of the class.

The fear, anguish, and despair of those early years were as visceral the day I took my son to kindergarten as they had been all those years ago. All that I had hoped to have left behind came rushing back, cascading down the trauma-lined synapses of my brain. So, it was with extreme pain that I saw my oldest son struggle, his eyes watering and his lower lip quivering. I saw my pain in him. My fear, hopelessness, and—above all—desire to be safe at home, knowing full well that was the one place I wouldn't be allowed to go.

But, as ever, there is sunlight after darkness. When I picked him up after school and saw his smiling face come around the corner, I was reminded of the staggering strength of our young people, these little humans in their little bodies navigating a world so large and loud. I was reminded, yet again, that life is struggle, and woe would it be for me to envision my role of father as he who spares my son the experiential power of struggle.

I knelt down to hug him. I squeezed him, looked in his eye, and said "You did it!"

"Yup!" he replied, with the infuriating and inspiring matter-of-factness of a five-year-old. We held hands as we walked home. I mined for the details of his day. And I envisioned that future day when my son held hands with a young child of his own, feeling the irrepressible heartache that is a parent's love for his child. (Wright, 2019/2018, Education Post, a platform of brightbeam)

Develop Hyperlocal Activism With Community-Run Equity Committees

There might be a tendency, when faced with enormous injustice, to find enormous solutions. But there are times when the smallest changes can have the largest impacts. This commitment to change on a small, local scale can be called *hyperlocal activism*. Start with a simple question: In your community, how are the children? Start digging into public data sets to get clues about their health and well-being. The free Civil Rights Data Collection (https://ocrdata.ed.gov) website allows you to gain deep insight into the students and community members who are being underserved. Using this database, schools can figure out if they are disproportionately disciplining students with disabilities, students of color, or English learner (EL) students and can juxtapose these findings against national averages to determine whether injustice is taking place and how much. These data sets can provide the necessary context for having important conversations that can galvanize true change at the individual school and at the district level in conjunction with social media pushes, follow-up emails, school board attendance, phone calls, letter-writing campaigns, and op-ed publications, which help effect real change (Ali, 2018; Cummings, 2018; Sister District Action Network, 2020).

Also in relation to these data resources, schools and districts need to engage family members and students in identifying areas of injustice and corresponding action steps. If, for example, a segment of the population has a disproportionate level of truancy, then it is incumbent on the district and school leadership to engage with the community to find out why. They can do that by sending out surveys, inviting families in for discussions, arranging home visits, and sending letters home to families in multiple languages. Districts then use input gained from families to create an intervention plan, track data to see if the plan is working, and report back to families either on progress or new interventions.

Schools and districts can facilitate dialogue by establishing community-run equity committees facilitated by families, caregivers, student representatives, teachers, and administrators. These equity committees can exist at both the school and district levels. After thorough community outreach and planning, committees should decide on multiple meeting times to accommodate diverse work schedules and wide-ranging accessibility measures to ensure no voices are left out due to ability. By ensuring that they bring as many voices to the table as possible, and that the voices of those for whom advocates are fighting are actively sought out and listened to, equity committees can become truly revolutionary.

After identifying issues and areas of injustice to tackle, the committees can break up into smaller subcommittees, each responsible for creating measurable action steps to address its specific issue. For example, one subcommittee could focus on ensuring all classroom libraries are diverse and empowering for all student identities; another could focus on disciplinary disparities across races, languages, and special education diagnoses; and a third could focus on differing outcomes among local elementary schools and their impact on students' success once they reach high school. In this way, a wide variety of community voices can come together, identify key issues, and create community-based solutions to address community concerns.

Ensure All Schools Have a Solid Tiered Support System

Nearly one out of every six children in America live in poverty, and nearly three out of every four children living in poverty is a child of color (Children's Defense Fund, 2021). Growing up in poverty is inextricably linked to experiencing trauma such as that ranging from food and housing insecurity to inadequate medical care to violence (Morsy & Rothstein, 2019). And while this trauma is acute, child trauma is a universal American problem (Substance Abuse and Mental Health Services Administration, 2021).

Students are suffering, living in chronic states of fear, anguish, withdrawal, and silence. One in five American children has been sexually molested; one in four has been beaten by a parent or guardian; one out of every three couples in America engages in physical violence; one out of every four Americans has a relative battling alcohol or drug addiction; and one out of every eight American children has seen their mother be the victim of physical violence (van der Kolk, 2014). So many students living with trauma go to school and are unable to learn. In many cases, teachers simply have no idea what trauma is doing to the students sitting in their classes.

Naturally, the options for addressing trauma's effects vary widely. Therefore, to ensure they serve, honor, and support all students, all schools should utilize a multitiered system of supports (MTSS) or response to intervention (RTI). The following explains the tiered approach (Buffum, Mattos, & Malone, 2018).

- Tier 1 is where educators cover grade- and course-level instruction; all students, regardless of whether they receive Tier 2 or Tier 3 interventions, should have full access to Tier 1 instruction.

- Tier 2 supports students who are missing certain specific skills necessary to succeed with grade- or course-level instruction and are generally delivered by a student's classroom teacher or member of that teacher's collaborative team. This could include reading supports, 1:1 supports, brain breaks, or any in-class focused support.

- Tier 3 includes remediation for students lacking foundational skills going back multiple grade levels that inhibit their ability to absorb grade- or course-level instruction. This could include pull-out services (while still maintaining Tier 1 access) for therapy or self-contained special education classrooms.

Effective use of the RTI model mandates universal screening or testing, intervention implementation, and progress monitoring. Because of the intricacies of this work, school counselors are essential (Belser et al., 2016). In an effective RTI program, schools can shift their focus and expertise away from punitive responses to student behavior and toward responses of understanding, empowerment, and love.

To ensure that all schools can effectively implement RTI, school funding formulas need to ensure that schools have a *counseling coordinator*: an expert in the field of student support and mental health who will be the source of answers, strategies, and resources for parents, families, and teachers alike. Without such a steward, families, students, and teachers find themselves lost in a sea of turmoil. For more about funding formulas, see chapter 2 (page 29).

In addition, all schools must have a budget that allows for the recommended student-to-counselor ratio of 250:1 (National Association for College Admission Counseling [NACAC] & American School Counselor Association [ASCA], n.d.). The average ratio is closer to 482:1, and in a handful of cases, states have ratios of more than 600:1 (NACAC & ASCA, n.d.). It is imperative that policy makers and legislators ensure that school budgets receive ample dollars to hire the school counselors needed to support our nation of children living with trauma.

It is important here to start small and local. First, use the Civil Rights Data Collection (https://ocrdata.ed.gov) to find the number of counselors available in a school and see what the ratio is of students to counselors. If the ratio is higher than 250:1, and it probably will be, then a multitiered response must take place. Contact the principal, assistant principals, superintendent, and board of education members. Use social media to shine a light on the inadequate number of counselors. Contact both state and local representatives. Publish op-eds in local news outlets.

 Lighthouse Beacon: *Zakiya Sankara-Jabar and Racial Justice NOW!*

Zakiya Sankara-Jabar didn't choose activism work; the work chose her. When her three-year-old son was suspended from his preschool, she came face-to-face with the preschool-to-prison pipeline. The data she had known so well personally in her research on systemic injustice had come to life.

Sankara-Jabar says she understands the overrepresentation of Black and Latinx students in special education and the underrepresentation of those same students in honors and Advanced Placement courses (Quinton & National Journal, 2014; Z. Sankara-Jabar, personal communication, March 15, 2021) as manifestations of the centuries-old idea of preventing Black children from learning. She sees children punished and suspended and taught to hate school and then labeled as not wanting to learn and not valuing education. For her, all systemic injustices come from the same place: anti-Blackness.

Sankara-Jabar has worked for educational justice at the local, state, and federal levels. She is the national director of activism at brightbeam (https://brightbeamnetwork.org), and she and Vernellia Randall started the nonprofit Racial Justice NOW! (https://rjnohio.org), an organization committed to dismantling structural and institutional anti-Black racism. She sat down directly with parents in Dayton, Ohio, and heard their desire for a change of curriculum and disciplinary practices. Sankara-Jabar and these families forced Dayton Public Schools to cease suspending elementary school and preschool students despite the opposition of teachers' unions and fought for restorative justice practices in the schools that had the greatest number of suspensions. Using restorative justice practices means that rather than simply removing a student from the school community, schools bring together students to promote repair and reconciliation (Seiki, 2019).

Sankara-Jabar says the results were staggering (personal communication, March 15, 2021). Once restorative practices took precedence over punishment, academic achievement jumped. Before, nobody was talking to the students to figure out what was wrong. They were just suspending students. With the restorative justice model, the schools didn't kick out students; they helped students calm down, connected with them, and supported them.

At the state level, Sankara-Jabar and her coalition convinced Ohio schools to ban suspensions and expulsions for students in preschool to grade 3, and at the federal level, she worked to ensure parent and guardian voices were included in the Every Student Succeeds Act (2015).

Sankara-Jabar says she depends on her village and encourages any people who fight against systems of injustice to build coalitions to take on the systems, which are larger and older than any single individual (personal communication, March 15, 2021). While building these coalitions, she never loses sight of her own self-care. This is heart work—work that is emotionally taxing and draining, with many sleepless nights and tear-filled days. But we must never give up.

Reflection Questions

Now that you have read this chapter, please consider the following questions. After reflecting alone, and then reflecting with a team if you are doing a book study, consider what actions you can take today. Who can you contact? What information can you research? Whose voice needs to be heard? What work needs to be done, and how can you be a part of it?

- What story of race in America is told in your school community? What impact does this choice have on students?

- How much work have you personally done to think about your benefit from and perpetuation of racism in America? How much work do you think teachers and administrators in your school community have done to this end?

- What steps is your local school community taking to develop culturally responsive teaching? What steps are you taking to become more culturally responsive?

- What patterns do the texts have that students in your local school community are reading in class? What culturally diverse texts aren't they reading, and why not?

- What are the disciplinary data for your school community according to the Civil Rights Data Collection (https://ocrdata.ed.gov)? What disciplinary disparities exist?

School Funding, Zip Codes, and Housing

2

Education in America is intended to be what is known as a *public good*. A public good is a government-provided service for benefit of all of its people without restriction. Typical public goods are national defense and infrastructure. To be a true public good, education should be non-excludable—available to all—and non-rivalrous (Stanford Encyclopedia of Philosophy, 2021). The truth is that education is not a public good and never has been in America. Education is a commodity—a good that is bought and sold on the marketplace with the greatest quality available solely to those who can afford the cost of admission.

Consider a 2018 nationwide study that reveals districts that have the highest poverty "receive about $1,000 less per student than the lowest poverty districts. The differences are almost twice as large—roughly $1,800 per student—between districts serving the most students of color and those serving the fewest" (Morgan & Amerikaner, 2018, p. 4). In short, the students who need the most get the least, and the students who have the most get even more. The students who have the greater probability of experiencing trauma are served by the schools with the fewest resources. What follows, then, is a self-perpetuating cycle. Students raised in families living in poverty attend under-resourced schools, do not gain the skills or knowledge necessary for higher-paying employment, cannot afford to move into a wealthier, greater-equipped school district, and ultimately must send their own children to a similarly under-resourced school—all of this because education in America is a commodity.

Market analyses show that "for a 1 standard deviation increase in test score, the price of a house increases by 1.93 percent or by $3,824" (Dougherty et al., 2009,

p. 538), meaning that the higher the test scores relative to the national average, the more expensive the school district. Other analyses demonstrate that housing in school districts with high test scores carries other economic implications besides increased housing value, among them "lower levels of perceived risk . . . higher expected price appreciation and enhanced liquidity . . . [and] lower price volatility" (Beracha & Hardin, 2018, p. 87). In short, parents of privilege are willing to pay high premiums for access to quality education. The commoditization of American education, compounded with the nefarious legacy of federally sanctioned residential segregation, has created and perpetuated a multitiered system where neighborhoods of wealth with fully resourced schools are also, not coincidentally, predominantly White, while neighborhoods of poverty with under-resourced schools are, again not coincidentally, predominantly neighborhoods of color.

This commoditization is not solely reserved for private, parochial, or public charter schools. Indeed, all traditional public schools are commodities bought and sold on the market, not in tuition payments but in mortgage payments. A quick look at any real estate website or app reveals the seemingly inextricable link between schools and homes. Alongside the square footage and numbers of bedrooms and bathrooms, you find the local school district, often with an attached school rating, such as the rating found on the popular website GreatSchools.org (www.greatschools.org), which uses a plethora of data to rate school districts as well as individual schools. For American families that are able to choose, the school to which a home is zoned plays a huge role in where they decide to live.

Adam Goldstein and Orestes P. Hastings (2019), assistant professors of sociology at Princeton University and Colorado State University respectively, note that "the fact that school attendance is coupled with neighborhood location makes residential choices a linchpin in parents' efforts to reproduce or advance the social class positions of their children," most notably in their access to quality education (p. 416). American families of means will spend as much as they can to live in a desirable school district. With any commodity in capitalist America, the greater a product's desirability, the greater the price. In fact, "most studies estimate the school premium to be somewhere on the order of [a] 2 percent to 10 percent" increase in housing cost (Goldstein & Hastings, 2019, p. 420). The result is a self-perpetuating system of economic and social self-segregation where those who can purchase their way into schools populated by other equally wealthy families do so. This is how the system functions and how the system was designed, but that does not mean this is the system that has to remain.

The following sections tackle these topics: school funding and zip codes, federal housing policy, integration, and so-called good schools.

School Funding and Zip Codes

The link between school funding and local wealth is one of the most pervasive perpetuators of educational injustice in America (Conlin & Jalilevand, 2015; Mahoney, 2013). While there is a certain of level of variability from state to state, in general, the majority of dollars funding American schools come from local property taxes. (Alexander, Salmon, & Alexander, 2015).

The result is schools in poor communities with low property tax values being severely under-resourced, while wealthy communities enjoy fully resourced schools. To compound this injustice, "most school finance systems require taxpayers in the less fiscally able school districts to exert several times more tax effort than that of the more fiscally able districts if they are to provide equal resources for their children" (Alexander et al., 2015, p. 66). As an example, take two communities, one wealthy and one impoverished. Assume the wealthy community's median household income is $151,000 and has an average property tax of $15,000. The impoverished community's median income is $27,015 with an average property tax of $1,278. While it may seem that vastly more money is spent in the wealthier community, those living in a wealthier community have the financial ability to pay those higher prices than those living in poverty. A median family in the wealthier community, after paying even the extraordinarily high property taxes of $15,000 per year, is still left with more than $130,000 of income—more than four times the amount of money of families living in the impoverished community who, after paying their property taxes, are left with about $25,000 in household income. This phenomenon is pervasive across the United States (Alexander et al., 2015).

The inequities in school district budgets cover the entire range of school experience, from teacher salaries and professional development to the length of the school day, class sizes, student support services, extracurricular activities, food, and transportation services (Morgan & Amerikaner, 2018). Schools with less funding have less money to hire teachers, so have more students per class. They have older technology, fewer extracurricular offerings, cheaper and less nutritious food, older busses, and older, more run-down infrastructures (Semuels, 2016). Thus, discussing the gaps in educational funding means discussing the entire school experience for students, families, and teachers.

A student in Philadelphia—the poorest big city in the country, with one of the largest school districts—is apportioned roughly $14,000 for K–12 education (Brubaker, 2020). Just west of the city, across the dividing line of City Line Avenue, a student in Lower Merion Township—an affluent, predominantly White suburb—receives roughly $28,000 for K–12 education (Brubaker, 2020). This disparity is the result of the formulas that equate housing value and local property tax wealth with school funding.

Why does per-pupil spending matter? Studies show that a "10% increase in per pupil spending . . . leads to 0.31 more completed years of education, about 7% higher wages, and a 3.2 percentage point reduction in the annual incidence of adult poverty" (Jackson, Johnson, & Persico, 2016, p. 157). Other research has similarly revealed that "students exposed to $1,000 more spending were 3 percentage points more likely to enroll in college and 2.3 percentage points more likely to earn a postsecondary degree" (Hyman, 2017, p. 256).

The numbers alone are sufficient to highlight the gross inequities of the system, yet the inequity is even greater than at first glance due to the fact that the communities with less funding are the communities that need more resources to offset the impacts of poverty. By some analyses, poor communities require 40 percent more funding than communities not living in poverty (Morgan & Amerikaner, 2018). Why? Because students living in poverty often require special remediation classes (Jiminez, Sargrad, Morales, & Thompson, 2016). These could be special classes, push-in supports, virtual instruction, homebound instruction, or any other number of supports. All these dollars are needed simply to match the quality education of those enjoyed by the wealthy.

Benefits of increased per-pupil spending are even greater for students living in poverty. In fact, studies go so far as to argue that a "25% increase in per pupil spending throughout the school-age years could eliminate the attainment gaps between low-income and non-poor families" (Jackson et al., 2016, p. 214). Educational justice, therefore, is not simply a case of throwing more money at a problem in hopes that it works. Educational equity is a known quantity.

How did American neighborhoods and school districts become so economically stratified? How are impoverished communities with under-resourced schools blocks away from affluent communities with fully resourced schools? The answer is residential segregation.

Federal Housing Policy

In myriad ways, the United States encouraged, incentivized, and enforced housing and mortgage lending policies aimed at maintaining racial segregation before and after the *Brown v. Board of Education of Topeka* (1954) decision, directly influencing significant educational injustices that continue to reverberate throughout the country.

Richard Rothstein's (2017) *The Color of Law* is indispensable to understanding the history and perpetuation of segregating housing policies in the United States. Rothstein (2017) makes it clear that segregation is not *de facto*—it doesn't just happen. Segregation is *de jure*—politically constructed by law, albeit often with race-neutral language that is routinely unenforced (Loh, Coes, & Buthe, 2020). Rothstein (2017) claims that these policies created "a nationwide system of urban ghettos, surrounded by white suburbs" (p. xiii). At the center of this system is the Federal Housing Administration (FHA) and an army of real estate agents leveraging racism into profits.

The free market didn't dictate housing segregation. The systematic and predesigned nature of mortgage lending, in addition to racists' violence and intimidation, is what created racially exclusive enclaves. Among the easiest and most effective ways to create legally segregated communities was simply to deny mortgages along racial lines. Prior to the Fair Housing Act of 1968, the FHA, created in 1934 during the Great Depression, would refuse "to insure mortgages for African Americans in designated white neighborhoods . . . they also would not insure mortgages for whites in a neighborhood where African Americans were present" (Rothstein, 2017, p. 13). In other words, "the government was not following preexisting racial patterns; it was imposing segregation where it hadn't previously taken root" (Rothstein, 2017, p. 14). But mortgage lending, effective as it was, was just one tool at the FHA's disposal.

During the Great Depression, as part of President Franklin Roosevelt's New Deal, federal housing projects began to pop up across the country. These housing projects were constructed with racial segregation practices much the same way as the FHA conducted its lending (Loh et al., 2020). In determining what types of housing were to be built and for whom, the Public Works Administration implemented neighborhood composition rules that made it policy that "federal housing projects should reflect the previous racial composition of their neighborhoods. Projects in white areas could house only white tenants, those in African American areas could house only African American tenants" (Rothstein, 2017, p. 21). Communities that had been legally segregated during Jim Crow due to the racism of the Fair Housing Act of 1968 now remained segregated by the Public Works Administration.

After racially segregated residential neighborhoods were constructed, real estate agents nationwide engaged in what came to be known as *blockbusting*:

> A scheme in which speculators bought properties in borderline black-white areas; rented or sold them to African American families at above-market prices; persuaded white families . . . that their neighborhoods were turning into African-American slums . . . and then purchased the panicked whites' homes for less than their worth. (Rothstein, 2017, p. 95)

These real estate agents would then resell these properties for a profit to African American families (Rothstein, 2017). The downward-spiraling housing values, orchestrated by real estate agents, created and then perpetuated the idea that where Black people moved, economic decline followed. In essence, realtors played into White racism to purchase homes under the market value, then selling the homes they had purchased at a discount to Black families at above-market rates (Loh et al., 2020).

Integration

True justice is not ensuring that marginalized communities access quality education via being in the same classrooms as White students. True justice is ensuring that all students access quality education whether the school serves White students or not. Integration—forced re-enrollment of schooling to achieve racial diversity—is not a solution to America's rigged education system. As mentioned in chapter 1 (page 7), the underlying assumption, therefore, is that—whether students of color are moved into predominantly White schools, or White students are transitioned into predominantly Black or Brown schools—where White students go, quality education follows. This is not a solution. Rather, it's another example of racism being a key structure of America's broken education system. What's needed is true justice in the form of anti-racism.

Historian and National Book Award winner Ibram X. Kendi's (2019) essential work, *How to Be an Antiracist*, defines an *anti-racist* as someone who "expresses the idea that racial groups are equal and none needs developing, and is supporting policy that reduces inequity" (p. 16). An *assimilationist*, rather, is someone who "express[es] the racist idea that a racial group is culturally or behaviorally inferior and [supports] cultural or behavioral enrichment programs to develop that racial group" (Kendi, 2019, p. 16). With these definitions in mind, it is clear that integration, whereby proximity to Whiteness is understood as the path to educational equity, violates the anti-racist notion of all races being inherently equal. Integration is assimilationist because it rests on the foundational belief of racial hierarchy—so long as Black and Brown children sit alongside White children, they will receive educational justice.

This is not to say, of course, that having integrated schools is bad. Quite the contrary! Studies show that all students in diverse schools benefit both socially as well as academically (The Century Foundation, 2019). However, integration without addressing the core causes of systemic inequity is not dismantling a system but rather putting a bandage on the problem.

This is a difficult pill for many to swallow, particularly for those who consider themselves anti-racist. Even prior to 1954's *Brown v. Board of Education*, which deemed state-sanctioned segregation unconstitutional, White Americans (both in the North and South) have exercised their desire for self-segregating through the following.

- *White flight*, wherein affluent White families leave America's increasingly Black and Brown urban centers for the predominantly White suburbs (Logan, Weiwei, & Oakley, 2017)

- Private school tuitions that tacitly exclude nearly all families that cannot afford the costs of enrollment (Flanagan, 2021)

- Gifted programs and public magnet schools that see nearly all-White classes in otherwise integrated school systems (Howard, 2018)

It bears considering that perhaps the injustice of *Plessy v. Ferguson*, the 1896 Supreme Court decision allowing for state-sanctioned segregation, lay not solely in the separate but also in the equal. Of course, mandated, law-based segregation has no place in

America. But to focus only on the notion of separation while doing little, if anything, to address equality is merely window dressing that fails to achieve true educational justice and equity that would ensure all students, regardless of race, class, or zip code, access to high-quality education.

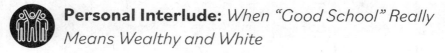

Personal Interlude: *When "Good School" Really Means Wealthy and White*

For most students, summer means the end of a school year, but for many it also means transition. Preschoolers transition to kindergarten, elementary students to middle school, and middle schoolers to high school. With transitions come decisions and, thanks to funding formulas that largely equate access to high-quality education with where one lives, parents often use these periods of transition to decide on where to settle, or re-settle, their families.

When this happens, particularly for young White progressives like me, the choices we make for our children run the risk of being at odds with our values. Indeed, when we were deciding what school district to choose for our family, my values of diversity, social justice, and anti-racism seemingly ran headlong into getting a "good" education for my children. But that whole idea of a "good" school can often simply be code for a school that serves a rich, White community, particularly when these "good" schools get high ratings on websites like GreatSchools.org.

GreatSchools.org is a treasure trove of information for families searching out the right school, but it also has the potential to incentivize self-segregation, particularly if parents equate a "good" school solely with overall ratings and test scores. Figure 2.1 has statistics for neighboring small-town school districts with one high school apiece: Haddonfield and Collingswood.

	Overall Rating	**Test Score Rating**
Haddonfield	8 / 10	8 / 10
Collingswood	4 / 10	5 / 10

Figure 2.1: High school overall ratings and test scores.

If I see these ratings, and *only* these ratings, then it is a no-brainer. There is little, if any, reason to choose Collingswood over Haddonfield, and there is substantial reason to choose Haddonfield over Collingswood. But test scores can be deceiving and there are other measures of academic achievement not shared on sites like GreatSchools.org. Figure 2.2 (page 36) shows graduation rates and college readiness for the high schools.

	Four-Year High School Graduation Rate	Average SAT Score	Average SAT Participation Rate	Percent of Graduates Pursuing a Four-Year College or Vocational Program	Percent of Graduates Pursuing a Two-Year College or Vocational Program
Haddonfield	98%	1262	100%	87%	6%
Collingswood	91%	1088	95%	42%	58%

Figure 2.2: Haddonfield and Collingswood High School graduation rates and after-school plans.

Readiness

There is a lot to unpack here. Graduation rates and SAT participation rates are relatively comparable in both districts, though admittedly there is a wider disparity in SAT scores. But the widest gulf is in what students choose to do after graduation. What could this mean? Why would Haddonfield's students go to colleges and universities to pursue bachelor's degrees at nearly double the rate of Collingswood's students, more than half of whom go on to pursue associate degrees? Judging from the similar graduation rates and relatively close SAT scores, this may not truly be about academics. Figure 2.3 shows relative wealth by comparing poverty rate, property value, and median household income in the two districts.

	Percent of Students From Low-Income Families	Median Property Value	Median Household Income
Haddonfield	2%	$492,500	$138,920
Collingswood	47%	$259,200	$64,885

Figure 2.3: Haddonfield and Collingswood compared by poverty rate, property value, and median household income.

Now things are getting clearer. In all likelihood, especially since graduation rates and SAT scores are relatively similar, the disparity in four-year college attendance has little, if anything, to do with academics or quality education. There is a disparity, however, in Advanced Placement (AP) courses, where according to school district data, 63 percent of Haddonfield students take an AP course versus 31 percent in Collingswood—though it is questionable how impactful these differences may be, particularly since simply enrolling in an AP course does not ensure passing the summative AP exam to earn college credit or ensure the class rigor.

Given the disparity in household income, the difference in four-year versus two-year college attendance between Haddonfield students and Collingswood students is likely just about what a student can afford, especially since the local state university costs $28,000 per year even for a commuting student, while the local community college costs less than $10,000 per year. One could even argue that going to the community college is the wiser decision since the degree conferred from the state university is identical whether a student started at community college or not. Essentially, a student who studied for two years at community college and then finished at the state university would have paid roughly $36,000 less than a student who spent all four years at the state university to earn the same degree. But let's go deeper. Figure 2.4 shows us more about these students.

	Percent of Students Who Are White	Percent of Students Who Are Black	Percent of Students Who Are Hispanic	Percent of Students Who Are Asian	Percent of Students Who Are Two-Plus Races
Haddonfield	89%	1%	3%	6%	2%
Collingswood	51%	21%	20%	5%	3%

Figure 2.4: Haddonfield and Collingswood High School student overview by ethnicity.

Now, we have a far clearer picture of whom these districts serve. Haddonfield is a wealthy, homogenous district, a bubble of White privilege where nearly all students have the financial ability to later attend a four-year college. Collingswood, by comparison, is a relatively diverse district, both in terms of race and socioeconomics, charged with serving students from different backgrounds, different cultures, and different needs. And still, nearly all students not only graduate, but go on to pursue postsecondary education.

The point is that if families trying to find the "good" school are looking solely at overall ratings and test scores, then "good" really means wealthy and White. If a family had only looked at Haddonfield's overall rating, for example, they would have chosen a profoundly segregated space for their children and done so because that's where the "good" schools were, when in fact Haddonfield could really be simply where the rich White people are.

But, if we look deeper and realize that education is more than test scores, but is also about embracing difference, learning from other cultures, and finding value in diversity both racial and economic, then our values do not have to be sacrificed for "good" education, particularly since Collingswood, while by no means perfect, may be the better choice after all due to its diversity, academic success, and cost of living.

These data points are available for any school district in the country. Families can access GreatSchools.org and cross-reference the data points found there alongside the data found at https://nces.ed.gov/ccd/districtsearch from the NCES. Then consider these questions: Which district would you choose, and perhaps more importantly, why? (Wright, 2019/2018, Education Post, a platform of brightbeam)

How to Make Change

Education has an inertia problem. Any type of educational reform runs into resistance. The call to agitate against the rigged system of education necessitates tireless activism for justice. The following sections focus on two areas—(1) litigation and (2) funding—and include both national and local actions that administrators and teachers can take. If education in America is to become just, the way schools are funded needs to radically change. District funding can no longer align with local property wealth. However, because the system as it is benefits the wealthy and powerful, it will be difficult to push school funding reform through state legislatures. That is why simultaneous action must be taken through the courts.

The following actions, explained in the following sections, explore how educators can make progress in classrooms and districts to address systemic inequities and racial injustices. These are not comprehensive or exhaustive, but they are starting points to create conversations and inspire action.

- Discover local funding realities.

- Litigate at the state level.

- Create a fair funding formula.

- Form equity coalitions.

Discover Local Funding Realities

The first thing teachers and administrators need to do to address inequitable funding formulas is to educate themselves on their own local funding realities. Teachers and administrators can access the NCES (n.d.d) Public School District Finance Peer Search database (https://nces.ed.gov/edfin/search/search_intro.asp) to identify funding disparities between districts within the states. This information is power, and teachers and administrators can use it to raise the alarm for their students and families and begin to mobilize by rallying for change at their local boards of education, writing op-eds for local news outlets, and creating social media petitions to agitate for change.

Litigate at the State Level

Navigating and agitating against entrenched school funding formulas is a herculean effort that, in my experience, requires wide coalitions and multiple points of attack. Policy makers cannot be relied on to fight for the work of the marginalized, under-represented, or traditionally excluded. It is therefore incumbent on teachers, administrators, families, and community members to become knowledgeable about funding systems and confident in not only saying what a just and equitable funding alternative looks like, but how to implement it.

State-level litigation that exposes inequitable school funding formulas as unconstitutional under state constitutions must be filed. In the absence of a federal constitutional right to an education, it comes down to the state courts to protect the right to an education (Wong, 2018). Once a link between quality education and baseline funding costs has been established, the primer has been set to use the court system to create a truly equitable school funding system.

What would a just funding formula look like? The first thing to do when coming up with a fair funding formula is to arrive at the baseline dollar amount per pupil that would guarantee access to a quality education in the state. This dollar amount must be found at the state, rather than local, level. That helps ensure equity by preventing a lower baseline for students living in poverty than for those living in wealthier communities.

There are four common methods to reach this baseline dollar amount: (1) the professional judgment model, (2) the successful schools model, (3) the advanced statistical model, and (4) the adequate funding model. Each method has merits as well as flaws, as table 2.1 shows.

Table 2.1: Methods to Reach the Baseline Dollar Amount per Pupil Guaranteeing Quality Education

Method	Process	Potential Strengths	Potential Flaws
Professional Judgment Model			
This model draws on the collective opinions of professional educators to imagine a school prototype that possesses all the resources students would need, after which a dollar amount is attached to the prototype (Levin et al., 2018).	Educators imagine a fully resourced school and arrive at the hypothetical cost.	Leverages the on-the-ground expertise of educators who have thorough knowledge of what resources schools need	Has the potential for implicit biases to impact professional judgment, particularly when imagining a school for specific student populations
Successful Schools Model			
Rather than imagining what a successful school would have, this model identifies real-life successful schools and quantifies a dollar amount those schools used to achieve their success (Alexander et al., 2015).	Policy makers identify a real successful school and use its funding dollar amount as the baseline.	Leverages a real school with real successes that is likely fully resourced and ensures that dollar amount for all students	Has the potential for maintaining inequity by not providing enough resources for special needs, poverty, and trauma because a successful school may not have significant populations of students with those types of needs

continued ▶

Method	Process	Potential Strengths	Potential Flaws
Advanced Statistical Model			
This model tries to account for the seemingly innumerable variables between schools and communities to arrive at a dollar amount a school would need to be successful (Alexander et al., 2015).	Educational researchers and statisticians use econometric modeling methods that isolate factors that contribute to school cost and student success to account for variables across communities to arrive at a baseline dollar amount.	Leverages advanced statistics to arrive at common dollar amounts for all districts	Has the potential for overlooking realities due to relying on researchers and statisticians; also ignores the realities of specific district needs required for fair funding formulas
Adequate Funding Model (Pouncey, Ennis, Woolley, & Connell, 2013)			
This model utilizes the latest research to account for what a theoretical school would need, and then uses the opinions of professional educators to decide whether that dollar amount is adequate.	Educational academics use the latest research to construct a hypothetical school, and then use educators' professional judgment to arrive at a dollar amount.	Combines the benefits of the professional judgment model and the advanced statistical model	May not account for the potential for implicit biases and still has the potential to not provide enough resources for communities living in poverty, with trauma, or with special needs

The advanced statistical model and the adequate funding model, although assuredly mathematically impressive, have the potential pitfall of not being thoroughly fluent in educational practices because they do not involve the expertise of educators and school leaders. That leaves the professional judgment model and the successful schools model.

The professional judgment model, although it certainly benefits from educators' expertise, runs the risk of being beholden to those educators' biases. In imagining a school, educators would likely envision the student population for whom their school would be built, and such imaginings invite the biases of what that particular school community deserves. A predominantly White, relatively wealthy group of educational experts, for example, might underestimate the costs necessary for adequately educating predominantly impoverished or non-English-speaking communities, a problem that could be mitigated by including school stakeholders such as students, families, and family liaisons. Understanding that not all schools that service predominantly students of color are in areas of poverty, the successful schools model would likely look to wealthy, predominantly White districts for models of successful schools, while ignoring the fact that such schools may not devote resources to serve communities living in poverty.

While using the dollar amount of these successful schools as a baseline would certainly close the funding gaps between rich and poor districts, it would not necessarily account for the needs of special populations, and could fail to account for differences in school performances across state lines.

Create a Fair Funding Formula

What is needed, then, is a two-part process that uses both the professional judgment model and the successful schools model, where the higher amount would become the new baseline dollar amount guaranteed to all students in the state (Alexander et al., 2015). After using the successful schools model to determine the baseline dollar amount at the national level, individual district and school funding pools can determine the state and local levels by multiplying the baseline dollar amount by the total number of students in the district or school. However, while this would create an *equal* funding formula, it would not create an *equitable* funding formula. Any family whose children benefit from more educational dollars because of a system that denies other children those same dollars is not enjoying a right. When some families protest, saying that new funding formulas are unequal, they are correct. They're not equal. They're equitable.

To create an equitable funding formula, specific categories must be created that apportion specific student populations with dollar amount increases on top of the baseline dollar amount to fit those specific student populations' needs. These funding categories include the following.

- A poverty supplement with a specific per-student addition for every baseline dollar; for example, if every school receives $18,000 per student, increase that number by 1.3 percent for every student living in poverty.

- A special education supplement with a specific per-student addition for every baseline dollar; for example, if every school receives $18,000 per student, increase that number by 1.5 percent for every student qualified for special education.

- An English learning supplement with a specific per-student addition for every baseline dollar; for example, if every school receives $18,000 per student, increase that number by 1.5 percent for every student qualified as an English learner.

- A preschool supplement to offer free universal preschool by either budgeting $5,500 per student to fund public preschool or to pass on these dollars to families to select a preschool of their choice

- An adverse childhood experience (ACE) supplement with a specific per-student addition for every baseline dollar; for example, if every school receives $18,000 per student, increase that number by 2 percent for every student with an ACE score of 5 or above. The ACE quiz is a way of quantifying childhood trauma such as abuse, neglect, or household dysfunction. While a high ACE score does not necessarily guarantee a life filled with suffering, trauma does impact the brain's ability to learn, thereby necessitating greater educational resources (Starecheski, 2015).

Some, predominantly the wealthy and privileged, may cry foul, arguing that for students from poverty, students with special needs, or students living with trauma to receive greater school funding is unequal. Indeed, "taxpayers in suburban enclaves see their economic advantage of residing in an affluent, property-rich suburb as an existing right" (Alexander et al., 2015, p. 132). All students will get what they need, rather than the status quo wherein the only students who get what they need are those who can pay for it. As arts education nonprofit board member Franklin Leonard (2015) has most famously said, to the privileged, equity feels like oppression when, in fact, it's justice.

Anybody who says funding schools at these levels is too expensive is wrong. When the United States spends $725 billion yearly on national defense (Peter G. Peterson Foundation, 2021) and the ultra-rich spend millions of dollars on joy rides into space (AFP, 2021), the problem isn't a lack of money, but a lack of interest in investing in the nation's children. It is up to teachers, school administrators, families, and activists to hold representatives and policy makers accountable and demand they show the will and courage to insist on fully funding America's schools.

Form Equity Coalitions

Teachers and administrators from under-resourced districts can partner with teachers and administrators from similarly under-resourced districts across their state to form equity coalitions that cut across school district boundaries, county lines, and political party affiliations to combat common injustices. While these partnering districts may look vastly different in terms of demographics, their common experience of being on the losing end of funding can create powerful lobbying blocs in state legislatures. Just imagine teachers, school leaders, families, and activists bussing into state capitols from the under-resourced cities, suburbs, farmlands, and rural areas, allied in demanding equitable school funding. That is political power at work.

In Pennsylvania, for example, while urban school districts like Philadelphia and Pittsburgh are in many ways the opposite of districts in rural areas like Erie, Altoona, and Punxsutawney (per Future Ready PA Index at https://futurereadypa.org/#), all districts suffer from inequitable educational funding based on the state formulas that equate local property wealth with local school funding. If all similarly under-resourced districts formed teacher and administrator equity coalitions, the power they could take to the statehouse would make any state legislator pause.

 Lighthouse Beacon: *Maurice Cook and Serve Your City*

Maurice Cook captures your attention immediately. His eyes and voice smolder with passion, anger, and purpose. Growing up in Maryland and Washington, DC, Cook founded Serve Your City (www.serveyourcitydc.org) in 2009 to provide immense support for the community he loves.

During the COVID-19 pandemic, Cook and his organization stepped up to provide necessities for his community, including $30,000 worth of food, 400 backpacks filled with laptops, internet hot spots, tens of thousands of masks, hand sanitizer, gloves, face shields, and free virtual tutoring to students in DC, Maryland, and Virginia, with 260 tutors working with 130 students, spending nearly 1,300 hours on video calls, all of which are free to kids. Cook and his organization have literally saved lives.

A self-described *have-not*, Cook grew up seeing others have more, and it changed him (M. Cook, personal communication, March 15, 2021). He saw the commodification of everything, even the basic necessities families need simply to survive. He saw that even for those with relative comfort, all it would take was a lapse of one or two paychecks for them to sink into poverty. This constant need to fight for basic survival, says Cook, is precisely what keeps systems of injustice up and running, for if folks must work tooth and nail to simply earn the basics to survive, they have nothing left to fight against the systems that necessitate those struggles in the first place. Cook's Serve Your City is a response to those systems that serves to level the playing field and close the gap between the haves and the have-nots.

When asked how others can do similar work in their own communities, Cook, without hesitation, says the first step is to build a team because impactful activism is too big for any single individual. Prospective activists also need to be honest with themselves; this work is taxing and depleting and requires significant sacrifices in time, money, relationships, and personal well-being. To be an activist and an educator requires knowing when to take the time to fill your cup and take care of yourself. Only by having a team and by practicing self-care can activists and educators stay in the game long enough to have consequential impact.

While Cook is angered by the fact that his work is even necessary in the first place, nothing compares to the joy he feels seeing a student receive a laptop, a family receive groceries, or a child learn to swim. Cook sees himself as a gardener, nurturing shoots in a forgotten garden (M. Cook, personal communication, March 15, 2021). Take heart. Change is possible, but only if we, like Cook, have the courage to stand up, show up, and fight for justice.

Reflection Questions

Now that you have read this chapter, please consider the following questions. After reflecting alone, and then reflecting with a team if you are doing a book study, consider what actions you can take today. Who can you contact? What information can you research? Whose voice needs to be heard? What work needs to be done, and how can you be a part of it?

- What makes a school good? How should parents, families, teachers, school leaders, and activists determine what a good school is?
- What resources do schools need to be effective? How much would those resources cost?
- What choices did you or would you make in terms of where to send children you love to school? Why?
- Is integration an effective method for educational equity? Why or why not?
- Should some students receive more for their education than others? Why or why not? And if so, who?

3

Teacher Preparation

When someone asks students what they want to be when they grow up, what do they often say? Professional athletes, doctors, lawyers, nurses, engineers, mechanics, astronauts, paleontologists, software designers, musicians, actors. What do they rarely say? Teachers.

Being a teacher isn't glamorous; it comes with no big paycheck, no social media status, and no clout, and anybody who says the summer vacation is a draw has never taught a class, let alone six periods a day, five days a week, for nine months a year. Nobody goes into teaching for the money. Indeed, while the average teaching salary has increased since 1993 to the tune of $56,383 total annually, these increases have risen far slower than inflation has (Alexander, 2020). To put it another way, "if a school teacher is the sole source of income for a family of four in South Dakota or Mississippi, her/his child would qualify for federal reduced-price meals as a student" (Alexander et al., 2015, p. 248).

If a profession's value is measured by pay, then teaching is simply not valued in America. Relatively lower pay than other professions combined with reported lack of support and prolonged stress has led to near perennial lack of qualified educators (Hester, Bridges, & Rollins, 2020). Teachers reporting being overworked is not hyperbole. Indeed, American teachers spend on average forty-six hours a week teaching—far more than the worldwide average of twenty-eight hours per week (Camera, 2019). Teaching, therefore, is an alternative profession, a job for those who are either altruistically inclined, financially secure, or unable or unwilling to pursue more lucrative professions. After all, from a purely economic vantage point, why would anybody go to college, accrue mountains of student loan debt, and then enter a teaching workforce, which will do little to financially offset such an investment? Understanding these economic disincentives to becoming a teacher helps explain America's chronic teacher shortages (Carothers, Aydin, & Houdyshell, 2019).

But the problems with how America enlists, prepares, and retains teachers go deeper than simply not being able to recruit teachers. Inequitable distribution of effective teachers is a key factor in America's broken education system. Indeed, the most under-resourced schools with the greatest need for highly trained, experienced, and effective teachers are far more likely to have novice, inexperienced teachers than their wealthier counterparts (Iasevoli, 2018). This is in part due to cost. Experienced and effective teachers are valuable; therefore, they can be more readily recruited by wealthy districts that have the resources to spend upwards of 70 percent of their budgets on teachers (NCES, 2020).

Under-resourced districts cannot afford the high salaries needed to attract the most experienced and effective educators. Some of these wealthier districts pay close to double what under-resourced districts can offer. In one of the wealthiest suburban districts outside Philadelphia, for example, the average teacher salary is upwards of $100,000 (Trinacria, 2017) while in neighboring Philadelphia, the average teacher salary is $56,000 (PayScale, n.d.). Consequently, there exists a revolving door of new teachers who ineffectively teach the student populations already underserved by a systemically unjust education system. The injustice is not only that America underappreciates teachers in general, but that the most experienced teachers are attracted to teach at the wealthiest districts who can afford to pay them higher salaries, while impoverished districts must hire novice educators who lack the adequate training and experience to serve struggling students who need the best teachers.

The following sections tackle these topics.

- Teacher training
- Teacher accountability

Teacher Training

To fully understand the degree to which America's method of teacher training is broken, as well as to imagine how to create more just systems, it is worth diving into the intricacies of how most teachers become fully licensed educators. Most people who become teachers in America go through state college and university education programs (NCES, n.d.a). They either major in education and minor in the subject area they plan to teach or major in the subject area and minor in education (Darling-Hammond & Lieberman, 2012). Increasingly, however, people in the United States are taking alternative pathways into the teaching profession. Often run by accredited programs, but not necessarily colleges or universities, these pathways are often of shorter duration and less expensive (Darling-Hammond & Lieberman, 2012). Some research indicates a small but significant difference in preparation quality between alternative and traditional programs, with alternative programs having slightly higher levels of teacher achievement (Whitford, Zhang, & Katsiyannis, 2018), though this is far from conclusive.

Regardless of what path they take into the profession, most educators who aim to teach in public schools (and most charter, private, or parochial schools) need to pass a set of standardized exams called the *Praxis*. These tests, created and given by Educational Testing Service—the same test maker responsible for the SAT—often come in two parts. The Praxis I (or Core Academic Skills for Educators) assessments are reading, writing, and mathematics tests "designed to provide comprehensive assessments that measure the skills and content knowledge of candidates entering teacher preparation programs" (ETS, n.d.a). In addition, prospective teachers must take and pass the Praxis II (or Subject) assessments that "measure subject-specific content knowledge" (ETS, n.d.a). Sitting for both tests takes nearly eight hours and costs about three hundred dollars (ETS, n.d.b).

Like all standardized exams, the Praxis exams are powerfully entrenched gatekeepers that face harsh criticism of being unfair and ineffective (Barnum, 2017). Indeed, research can show little to no connection between a teacher's ability to effectively teach and the teacher's scores on standardized exams (Henry et al., 2013). Just as most patients don't measure their doctors' effectiveness based on what they scored on their licensure exams, the relationship between effective teaching and a high Praxis score is similarly dubious. What is known, however, is that these standardized exams are barriers against diversifying the education workforce in America.

Teacher Accountability

It is true that teachers in America are generally underpaid, under-trained, and underappreciated. It is also true, however, that America's teachers need greater accountability for providing high-quality education—particularly to poor and traditionally marginalized students. But teachers cannot be held accountable for providing high-quality instruction when they themselves have not been adequately trained. Crazy as it sounds, most teachers have not been taught how children learn to read (Hanford, 2018). How are teachers held accountable for student learning when their preparation doesn't include something as basic as reading instruction?

Teachers need a strong foundation in the theoretical aspects of education, but the practical aspects are just as important—those everyday teacher moves that too many teachers must learn on the fly, including how to stand and deliver instructions, how to set and reinforce expectations, how to use public and individual redirections, how to circulate through the classroom and collect data, and how to introduce new material and make lessons stick. Bottom line: high-quality teaching all starts with high-quality teacher preparation.

How to Make Change

It is common to look to worldwide education leaders to plot a course for American education reform. But there's a problem with this approach. America's size, heterogeneity, state-controlled education, and history prevent it from being able to simply emulate another country's education system. However, while the United States cannot magically transform its education system, there are specific best practices that districts and schools can adopt to make their education more equitable and just.

Generally, countries with strong education systems share the following traits (Darling-Hammond & Lieberman, 2012).

- A universal understanding of what good teaching looks like
- A sophisticated and advanced teaching corps with near-universal advanced-degree holdings
- Fully subsidized teacher preparatory programs that promote quality teaching and include extended paid teacher residencies
- Competitive salaries for teachers, on par with those of other professionals with advanced degrees

Along those lines, the following actions, explained in the following sections, explore how educators can make progress in classrooms and districts to address systemic inequities and racial injustices. These are not comprehensive or exhaustive, but they are starting points to create conversations and inspire action.

- Improve teacher residency programs.
- Ensure practice-based teacher preparation in authentic environments.
- Diversify the teacher pipeline.
- Incentivize becoming a teacher.
- Have teachers learn more about the communities they serve.

Improve Teacher Residency Programs

For far too many teachers, particularly those in under-resourced districts, schools provide new hires with insufficient on-ramping. Many teachers, myself included, pass a few tests, get a certification that allows them to teach while taking classes at night, and are thrown into a classroom. This system sets up teachers, schools, and most importantly, students and families for a lower-quality educational experience. The system doesn't have to work this way—particularly considering that the U.S. Department of

Labor's apprenticeship programs for many trades, including hospitality and cyberse-curity, can last up to four years (U.S. Bureau of Labor Statistics, 2013).

It is likely that less than 15 percent of teachers in America undergo a teacher resi-dency program (Loewenberg, 2018). To ensure that all teachers participate in teacher residency programs, all teacher preparatory programs must include, in the final year of their programs, a full year of teacher residency. This can be accomplished through relationships among teacher preparatory programs, school districts, and the National Center for Teacher Residencies (NCTR). NCTR (n.d.) has partnered with school districts across the country and seen impressive results, with more than 90 percent of residents outperforming traditionally trained teachers, 95 percent of residents report-ing that they were effectively prepared for their first year of teaching, 86 percent of residents continuing to teach in their first school for more than three years, and more than half of residents identifying as teachers of color. Teacher residency programs are the way to ensure a diversified and prepared corps of new teachers.

Improved teacher residency programs, although they have some detractors, are a desirable goal. In this scenario, teacher residents are placed in a school with a mentor teacher for an academic year. They are there every single day. While receiving intense instruction from the preparatory program, residents immerse themselves in the day-to-day rigors in their placement. During that full year, teacher residents will engage in a gradual on-ramp, beginning the school year observing their mentor teacher and slowly taking on more teaching responsibility. The gradual on-ramp, while not stan-dardized, empowers teachers to progress from teaching minilessons to leading one or two sections to leading a full class load with oversight and continuous feedback from an on-site professional. When compared to traditional student-teaching programs, in which prospective teachers engage in roughly four hundred hours of preservice teach-ing, residency programs have teachers tally upwards of nine hundred hours of teaching (Loewenberg, 2018), thus making their first year of full-time teaching actually more like their first two years. No doctor is thrown into the ER on day one, and if teach-ers are to be as effective as their students need them to be, none of them should get thrown into classroom instruction on their first day.

By the end of the academic year, a resident who receives a job offer to teach at the residency school will have a tool kit of strategies, competencies, and experiences that the resident developed in that school community. This will lead to increased cultural awareness and a first year of full-on teaching that won't be an excruciating trial by fire. Teachers' residencies ideally take place in the school where they are training to become full-time teachers, thereby empowering teacher residents with the ability to understand the culture of the school and begin to build relationships with students and faculty. Residents should receive stipends to support themselves during the year and should attend weekly practice sessions wherein their cohort reflects on common classroom issues and practices specific teaching strategies. This will help new teachers be effective during their first years in the classroom.

In addition, they might consider tapping into the resources offered by the NCTR (https://nctresidencies.org), a nationwide leader in the development of teacher residency programs. NCTR (n.d.) has recruited and prepared over 1,400 teacher residents and offers a way for families, district leaders, and teachers to begin creating teacher residency programs in their own areas. Families and teachers can push districts to begin partnerships, and district leaders can initiate partnership creation. This is the perfect place to start.

Ensure Practice-Based Teacher Preparation in Authentic Environments

There is no doubt that theory is important. However, far too many teachers' training includes theory alone. This is a setup. It is useless to learn theory in isolation from practice. What results is a near-universal experience for new teachers in the classroom: as they stand in front of an out-of-control classroom and think back on their prep programs, they can cite the latest theories and research, but they actually have no idea how to teach.

There is no one way to be an effective teacher. There is no one tone of voice, no one physical posture, no one teaching style that will result in all students learning. There are, however, some very basic teacher moves and practices that make a new teacher a better teacher faster. Table 3.1 includes a short list of best practices for new teachers. A full explanation of each strategy is beyond the scope of this book and so, where applicable, I suggest resources for learning more.

Table 3.1: Practical Classroom Procedures

Teaching Strategy	Description	Impact
Classroom Circulation	The teacher consistently moves through the classroom, rather than remaining at the front of the room (Lemov, 2015).	Classroom circulation increases student engagement in the classroom by minimizing the passive learning of lectures.
Proximity	The teacher moves next to students who appear distracted to nonverbally refocus their attention.	Proximity enables teachers to ensure students are engaged in lessons without resorting to invasive, embarrassing, and potentially combative public redirections.

Wait Time	When asking a question, the teacher waits three to five seconds, repeating the question before calling on a student.	Wait time allows students processing time and increases the likelihood of hearing multiple students' voices rather than just the voices of students who raise their hands the quickest.
Cold Calls	After wait time, the teacher calls on a student rather than calling for a volunteer (Lemov, 2015).	Cold calls can increase engagement as teachers randomly call on students rather than rely on raised hands. However, teachers should never use cold calls to embarrass students who may not be paying attention.
Warm Calls	Before asking a question and using wait time, the teacher signals or otherwise notifies students that they will be called on (Lemov, 2015).	Warm calls, similar to cold calls, can increase the engagement of student voices, but warm calls accommodate different student learning needs by giving students some preparation time before teachers call them.
Praise, Prompt, Leave	When a student appears distracted or off task, the teacher approaches the student, gets down to the student's level, praises an action, reminds the student what should be taking place now, and then leaves the student to circulate through the rest of the classroom (Lemov, 2015).	Praise, prompt, leave is a trauma-informed approach to supporting students who may be disengaged in learning due to coping with traumatic experiences (Jones, Jones, & Jones, 2007). Instead of criticizing or punishing students who are off task, teachers safely and supportively engage students on their physical level, offer praise, indicate next steps, and then leave the students to get back on track. The walking away conveys trust in the students and avoids a power dynamic where a teacher waits for a student to get to work, which invites conflict.
Positive Narration	While students are working on an assigned task, the teacher circulates and narrates the positive things students are doing (Lemov, 2015).	Positive narration simultaneously provides positive feedback for students and reinforces positive strategies and habits.

continued ▶

Teaching Strategy	Description	Impact
Clear Directions	When giving a set of directions, the teacher makes the directions short, sequential, and observable.	Clear directions mitigate student confusion, reinforce the feeling of trust between students and teachers (as teachers show they have practiced and fine-tuned their instructions), and create positive class momentum.
Turn and Talk	The teacher poses a question and has students turn to their neighbors to discuss it.	Turn and talk makes students, rather than the teacher, the center of the classroom action; it allows students to learn from one another and enables teachers to gather data as to what students are thinking.
Everybody Writes	The teacher poses a question and has students independently write a response in a short amount of time (Lemov, 2015).	Similar to turn and talk, everybody writes makes students, rather than the teacher, the center of the classroom action and enables teachers to gather data as to what students are thinking.
Gestures	The teacher uses hand signals or similar gestures for student responses. (For example, students who think the answer is A hold up one finger; students who think the answer is B hold up two fingers.)	Gestures are an efficient way for teachers to gather data on what students think, and they enable all student voices to be heard quickly and effectively.
Classroom Procedures	The teacher prepares, teaches, and reinforces procedures for common classroom issues, such as using the bathroom, transitioning to and from the carpet, and needing a pencil.	Well-thought-out classroom procedures ensure smooth class transitions that prevent wasted classroom time and mitigate distractions.
Standards-Based Lesson Planning	The teacher creates a daily lesson that includes a standard-aligned objective; a series of instructional delivery methods and activities that enable students to learn, practice, and master the given objective; a series of anticipated student misconceptions; and an assessment with a teacher-made exemplar (Lemov, 2015).	Effective lesson planning ensures that teachers are teaching students the most appropriate and important next piece of content, skill, or strategy. It also ensures that students are engaged and that teachers can gather data regarding students' mastery of the day's objective.

Teacher preparatory programs must not only teach future educators these best practices but also include significant time for teachers to authentically practice these teacher moves. The bottom line is that new teachers must try these strategies with students before they ever stand up in front of their own classrooms; otherwise, they will miss out on massive opportunities to be effective with their students. These strategies also need to be revisited and remastered by educators at all experience levels. Just as professionals practice the fundamentals of their craft, so must all teachers practice the fundamentals of effective instruction.

Experienced teachers need to also make time to pop in to observe their younger colleagues, not just to provide support and coaching, but also to learn new tricks of the trade. If educators see growth areas that could benefit all teachers and students, they should advocate for professional learning to develop those missing skills. Teachers can also join national professional communities of teachers in their specific subjects, such as the National Council of Teachers of English, the National Council for the Social Studies, the National Science Teaching Association, and the National Council of Teachers of Mathematics to collaborate and build new ideas. In short, teachers ideally never stop being students.

In addition to residency, teacher preparation is ideally grounded in, but not limited to, educational theory. Many teachers leave their teacher prep programs with a thorough and empowering knowledge of discovery learning, Maria Montessori (1995), B. F. Skinner (1947), Jean Piaget and Bärbel Inhelder (1969), and Lev S. Vygotsky (1934). This is important knowledge to be sure. But many of these same teachers left their programs without knowing what to do when nobody raised a hand to answer a question, or when ten students needed to sharpen pencils at the same time, or how to make classes more engaging, or how to figure out whether students have actually learned what was taught. Essentially, these teachers learned what teaching was about, but not how to do it.

Teacher preparation needs to include educators and coaches showing teachers how to teach, seeing them practice, giving them feedback, and ensuring those new teachers do it again, better. Feedback is the key and is what separates ordinary practice from what is known as *deliberate practice* (Clear, n.d.). While in ordinary practice, the person practicing is simultaneously trying to practice, observe, assess, and remediate, in deliberate practice the coach is responsible for observing, assessing, and remediating (Clear, n.d.). All the teacher has to do is practice, receive the feedback, and try again. This is how professionals master their craft.

Prep programs need to provide both theory and deliberate practice. Prep programs need to educate new teachers on foundational theory, *and* they need to ensure that teachers practice and master the moves that make up a teacher's bread and butter. Prep programs need to guide teachers to learn about the students and the communities they will serve so the teachers will do so with compassion, knowledge, and humility.

Teachers need to see maps of the cities and communities they serve. They need to know the demographics, the data, and the stories. They need to walk the streets, visit the corner stores, and talk with community leaders. When all of these things occur, then teachers on the first day of school can have a culturally responsive attitude toward students, a theoretical foundation for their practice, and answers for the ten students who all need to sharpen their pencils.

Diversify the Teacher Pipeline

As discussed in chapter 1 (page 7), a key element of America's broken system of education is the homogeneity of its teaching force. As the general population of the United States continues to become more diverse, with the majority of the population projected to be Americans of color by 2040 (Goings & Bianco, 2016), so does America's student population. Despite massive shifts in student demographics that have resulted in thirty-six of the country's largest metropolitan areas having a so-called *minority-majority* of young children (Mordechay, n.d.), America's teaching force remains more than 80 percent White (Goings & Bianco, 2016). Of the entire American teaching population, only 2 percent of teachers are Black males (Goings & Bianco, 2016).

This is a problem for all of America's students. For many students of color, having a teacher who looks like them is hugely important; it can signal a more nuanced understanding of culture and cultural expression, and lead to stronger teacher-student relationships and a greater sense of student belonging. In addition, teachers of color can be less likely to expel or suspend students of color or otherwise perceive them as threats (Partelow, Spong, Brown, & Johnson, 2017), a crucial factor given the wide disciplinary disparities found across the country (U.S. Department of Education Office for Civil Rights, 2014). Also, studies show that teachers of color often have greater expectations of their Black and Brown students than many White teachers do (Partelow et al., 2017). Teacher expectations have huge impact on student achievement; in fact, research shows that students taught by teachers with high expectations score significantly higher on school assessments than students taught by teachers with lower expectations (Papageorge, Gershenson, & Kang, 2020).

For students of color, most educational experiences involve windows—that is, education whose focus is outward, toward other communities (Bishop, 1990). Having teachers of color turn those windows, finally, into mirrors and seeing themselves as educators can be profound and edifying. Instead of learning through windows solely about peoples, histories, and stories to whom students of color can feel little to no connection, incorporating more diverse voices, histories, and perspectives can transform schooling into something meaningful that reflects student identities: mirrors.

Not just students of color benefit from having teachers of color. Far too few White students have ever had a teacher of color. In fact, nearly half of all schools in the United

States do not employ a single teacher of color (The 74, n.d.), and only one out of every five schools are led by an administrator of color (Hansen & Quintero, 2018). This type of racial isolation may breed intolerance, bias, and misunderstanding. In short, White students need to see fewer mirrors and more windows, and while it is not a teacher of color's job to guide White students down the path of racial awareness, such a journey is more likely to begin if teachers of color are in the school in the first place.

But there are roadblocks that need clearing. First, the American education system needs radical resource redistribution to ensure all students have access to a quality education so they can pursue and succeed in postsecondary education. As it stands, the high school graduation rate for Black males hovers just above 50 percent (Goings & Bianco, 2016), and based on research by the United Negro College Fund (n.d.), less than half of students were exposed to college-level courses in high school, thereby jeopardizing these students' success in college. Furthermore, roadblocks remain for those who do go on to complete college. As discussed earlier, the Praxis examinations (see page 47) represent solid gatekeepers into the teaching profession, with White teachers scoring higher than Black or Brown teachers (Goings & Bianco, 2016), thus creating another barrier into the profession for the teachers of color America so badly needs.

There are ways to create a diverse teacher pipeline in America. Activists and families can use tools created by the Education Trust (n.d.) to hold local and state-level officials accountable for creating plans to diversify the teacher pipeline. With the Education Trust's interactive diversity and equity tool (https://edtrust.org/educator -diversity/#US), which analyzes huge amounts of data, users can see how their state is doing in terms of creating data sets to analyze teacher diversity, creating teacher diversity goals, investing in teacher preparatory programs, intentionally recruiting prospective teachers of color, and improving teacher retention. After tapping into the data, district leaders can establish specific goals for diversifying their teacher workforce by creating partnerships with teacher residency programs; teachers can agitate for change by bringing the data to their school and district leaders; and families can petition their local schools and districts while writing op-eds and organizing social media groups around diversifying their teacher pipelines.

Incentivize Becoming a Teacher

If teaching remains a costly profession to enter with minimal financial reward, it will remain an underappreciated and understaffed career with underqualified personnel. The best and brightest will not go into teaching if they have to accrue significant student debt, study for and pass costly examinations, and then perform an immensely difficult job to make $45,000 per year (Alexander, 2020).

To attract the best and brightest into becoming America's next corps of educators, all teacher preparatory programs need to be heavily subsidized, and the universal starting salary for teachers must be $60,000 (Ringelstein, 2018). With this salary, teachers can pay off student debt, save to afford a home, and give their own families comfortable lives. Then, and only then, will teaching attract a more robust corps of young professionals and the profession can attain the level of professional respect it has so long lacked.

With such a stratified system of teacher pay scales that differ from district to district (let alone state to state), the most efficient and likely effective way to ensure teachers earn a base salary of $60,000 is by making it a federal policy. By some estimates, funding an annual base salary of $60,000 per year for 3.2 million teachers would cost less than $200 billion (Ringelstein, 2018) and would free local and state coffers to spend their dollars on other educational investments. With a federal budget of $6.82 trillion in 2021, America has the money to fund its teachers to help ensure a quality education for its children (USAspending.gov, n.d.).

Have Teachers Learn More About the Communities They Serve

Teachers do not have to live in the community in which they teach, but they need to demonstrate the willingness to learn about, support, and value the community they serve. A place to start is the Civil Rights Data Collection (https://ocrdata .ed.gov), which provides extraordinary amounts of data on schools and districts without attaching subjective value ratings. With this treasure trove of data, teachers can learn the following information.

- Student population demographics
- Teacher demographics
- Academic offerings
- Funding details
- Academic performance data
- Disciplinary data
- Graduation and postsecondary data

But this information is just a starting point. Data points, as important and powerful as they can be, cannot paint a holistic picture of a school community. Teachers must set foot outside the school building. To truly learn about and value a school community, during their residency, prospective teachers need to go to the local stores for lunch and coffee, get to know the crossing guards by name, and be able to navigate the streets on foot. New teachers can do some of the following.

- Eat lunch at local eateries including corner stores, food trucks, or food stands.
- Attend local sporting events, concerts, and other cultural events.

- Ask to attend block parties.
- Relax in the local park.
- Shop at the local businesses.
- Walk the neighborhoods.

Lighthouse Beacon: *Sharif El-Mekki and the Center for Black Educator Development*

Sharif El-Mekki is a force, transforming the landscape of American education. He is a former principal and teacher, former U.S. Department of Education principal ambassador fellow, and a U.S. delegate to the International Summit on Teaching and Learning and the Conference on Integrating Refugees and Immigrants Into Schools. In 2019, El-Mekki founded the Center for Black Educator Development (n.d.; www.thecenterblacked.org) "to ensure there will be equity in the recruiting, training, hiring, and retention of quality educators that reflect the cultural background and share common socio-political interests of the students they serve" (S. El-Mekki, personal communication, May 6, 2020). With professional learning for current Black teachers, pedagogical resources to develop social justice curricula, and a teacher pathways program designed to recruit Black high school–aged students to become educators, the Center for Black Educator Development is changing American education.

Pivotal to the Center for Black Educator Development's work is centering and prioritizing pedagogy crafted and honed by effective Black educators spanning generations. Traditional academia has largely ignored most of these educators in favor of the likes of John Dewey and Horace Mann, theorists who, while having much to offer, did much if not all of their work without any connection to the Black community. The Center for Black Educator Development therefore de-centers the Whiteness of educational theory by prioritizing works of Caroline LeCount, W. E. B. Du Bois, Marva Collins, Mary McLeod Bethune, Lucy Craft Laney, and various other educational theorists whose works should be on all teacher prep curricula.

By 2025, El-Mekki and the Center for Black Educator Development (n.d.) plan to support 250 elementary students with their network of Freedom Schools Literacy Academies, 100 Black high school students with taking dual-credit education courses, 50 Black college students with committing to teach after graduation, 25 Black college graduates with enrolling in local teacher residency programs, 25 Black students with receiving Black educator scholarships, and 50 early-career Black teachers with receiving mentoring by expert Black teachers. This is transformative work.

As my mentor, former school leader, and friend, Sharif El-Mekki has probably taught and inspired me more than any other person I've ever met. When I asked him what advice he would give to anyone who wants to work for justice, his reply was clear, honest, and challenging: (1) teach and (2) teach superbly.

Reflection Questions

Now that you have read this chapter, please consider the following questions. After reflecting alone, and then reflecting with a team if you are doing a book study, consider what actions you can take today. Who can you contact? What information can you research? Whose voice needs to be heard? What work needs to be done, and how can you be a part of it?

- If your child (or your niece, your nephew, or any other young person you care about) wanted to become a teacher, what would your honest response be, and why?

- How much do you think the average teacher salary should be? (After deciding, consider a babysitter who charges $12 an hour to watch one child. At that rate, a teacher with a class of thirty students—who, of course, is doing exponentially more work than a babysitter—who teaches six hours a day for nine months would make just under $400,000.)

- Considering the preparatory programs of other professions, such as lawyer, health-care provider, and accountant, how rigorous, exclusive, and time consuming should teacher preparatory programs be?

- How effective was your teacher preparatory program? How could it have been better?

- As a student, when was the first time you had a teacher of color? Have you ever had a Latinx teacher? A Black teacher? An Asian American or Pacific Islander teacher? What do your answers tell you about your educational experience?

4

Conflicts Between Reformers, Unions, and Schools

The 20th century American thinker Reinhold Niebuhr said, "Man will always be imaginative enough to enlarge his needs beyond minimum requirements and selfish enough to feel the pressure of his needs more than the needs of others" (as cited in Alexander et al., 2015, p. 73). This is definitely true in the fight over school funding.

Those who can live in affluent school districts, and benefit from the correspondingly abundantly resourced school districts, tend to fight against equitable redistribution of resources and come up with innumerable reasons to defend their privilege (Sattin-Bajaj & Roda, 2020). Among their reasons are the following (Alexander et al., 2015).

- "We have earned our wealth and the advantage that comes with it."
- "Our children have high aspirations and potential and therefore need fully resourced schools."
- "The costs of living in our area are higher, so our district needs more money."
- "Our school district is a model for others."
- "Our local school district is autonomous, and any state control would be an undue encroachment."
- "The poorer districts are filled with people who are poor because of choices they made, not because of something we did to them."

They back these notions of inequity as justice with the strong political capital that comes with wealth. While families in poorer, predominantly urban communities agitate for more equitable funding formulas, families in wealthier, predominantly suburban communities agitate to maintain the inequitable status quo (Sattin-Bajaj & Roda, 2020). It is no surprise that the wealthy communities, often with political connections and power, predominantly prevail in this struggle.

The following sections discuss the following ideas.

- Underfunded schools pitted against one another
- Teachers' unions versus school choic

The depth, ubiquity, and vitriol of the conflicts between these stakeholders is ironic given that these stakeholders could, and indeed must become powerful allies in the dismantling of America's broken education system.

Underfunded Schools Pitted Against One Another

In states with regressive funding formulas, among them Pennsylvania, where I am a teacher, schools in cash-strapped districts, starved for the dollars left over from the wealthy districts, fight among themselves for every leftover dollar. Developments in Pennsylvania illustrate this phenomenon. In 2020, Governor Tom Wolf pushed a charter school law that readjusted the budget formula so that $280 million was redirected from public charter schools—publicly funded, semi-autonomous public schools that must adhere to state testing and special education requirements but have greater say over the curriculum and the hiring and firing—back to traditional public schools (Hanna, 2020). Seventy thousand of Philadelphia's students attend brick-and-mortar public charter schools. That is one out of every three students in Philadelphia. And, on top of that already huge number, there are likely thousands more waiting for the chance to enroll. These aren't just numbers. These are students with families. For so many of these families, their neighborhood traditional public schools have, sometimes for generations, failed to live up to their charge of providing their families and students a quality education because of the funding systems.

All across the country, underfunded schools are pitted against one another for what is left behind by wealthier districts that benefit from classist and racist budgetary funding formulas. In Pennsylvania, budgetary funding makes it possible for a wealthy suburb to be able to devote $28,000 per student, while merely three miles away, a student in Philadelphia gets $14,000 (Pennsylvania Department of Education, n.d.).

Teachers' Unions Versus School Choice

Teachers' unions are political entities. While they may stand shoulder to shoulder with teachers outside of schools and purportedly fight for students, they are essentially political lobbying organizations at both the state and federal levels. Indeed, from 2004 to 2016, teachers' union donations increased from $4.3 million to $32 million (OpenSecrets, n.d.).

They have an even larger financial imprint at the state level. In 2008, New York City's United Federation of Teachers spent more than $6 million on lobbying and another $4.7 million in 2013, while in 2005, the California Teachers Association spent $58 million on state campaign initiatives (Campanile, 2015; Coulson, 2010). This spending by itself isn't necessarily a blemish on teachers' unions' reputations; indeed, in nations all over the world, strong teachers' unions align with strong educational performance (Darling-Hammond & Lieberman, 2012). However, it is important to understand unions for what they are: political lobbying organizations. Unionized teachers, therefore, must keep a close eye on the decisions made by those who purport to represent teachers nationwide to ensure that what is being advocated aligns with what is best for students.

Teachers' unions have used their substantial political power for the better in significant ways—for example, ensuring livable working wages for teachers. It is in large part due to the power of teachers' unions' collective bargaining agreement that public school teachers' average salary, including benefits, is $56,383 for traditional public schools (Alexander, 2020), significantly more than that for nonunion private school teachers. This is a vital victory and one that should not be overlooked or downplayed; indeed, as noted in chapter 3 (page 45), increasing teacher salaries is key to incentivizing the best and brightest to become teachers in the first place.

In other aspects, however, teachers' unions have positioned themselves in opposition to a fair, equitable, and anti-racist education system. Teachers' unions and their teachers who serve in America's traditional public schools enjoy a near monopoly on government funding, receiving almost $762 billion in annual education spending in 2018 alone (NCES, n.d.c). Unions are therefore extremely protective of this monopoly and fight infringement by using their considerable lobbying might against school choice initiatives, like public charter schools and vouchers, which would allow greater competition and different school options for families to choose from (National Education Association [NEA], n.d.b).

A common refrain of teachers' unions is that charter schools are an attack against public education, a privatization of what ought to be a purely public resource (NEA, n.d.a, n.d.b). The problem with this argument, as explained in chapter 2 (page 29), is that America's public education is already a market-driven commodity. Families of privilege use school choice all the time, sometimes in the form of tuition, but more so in their choice of whether to buy or to rent a home and thereby access the local school. A family choosing to reside in a desirable neighborhood is exercising the very same choice that less privileged families may make when choosing a charter school. Therefore, for teachers' unions to assert that charter schools are a danger to public education is misdirection. In fact, research concludes that some:

> Charter school students perform at a level equivalent to receiving an additional 22 days of learning in reading and 63 days in math per year when compared with their public school counterparts. The results for students attending schools associated with a Charter Management Organization were even greater, adding up to approximately 57 additional days in reading and 103 in math. (Goode, 2017)

Teachers' unions' narrative of defending public education isn't about public education at all—it's about turf. If teachers' unions truly want to make American education the public good it ought to be, they will fight not against charter schools and family choice but against regressive funding formulas. This is not to say that charter schools are perfect. They are not. Some charter schools choose specific students they want, much like public magnet schools do, with exhaustive application processes and strict admission guidelines (Simon, 2013). Anybody who uses a definitive statement that begins with "Charter schools are . . ." is either intentionally misleading or uninformed.

How to Make Change

There is strength in numbers, and while so much activism work is about building these numbers into coalitions, teachers' unions and education activists have, at their disposal, millions of teachers, millions of dollars, and access to policy makers in every corner of the country from the district level to the halls of Congress. To dismantle America's broken education system, all those who fight and agitate for students and families must come together, find common ground, and do what is best for children.

The following actions, explained in the following sections, explore how educators can make progress in classrooms and districts to address systemic inequities and racial injustices. These are not comprehensive or exhaustive, but they are starting points to create conversations and inspire action.

- Reprioritize teachers' unions' missions.
- Cease fighting school choice.
- Mobilize parents and families.

Reprioritize Teachers' Unions' Missions

Teachers' unions are essential to ensure teachers are adequately compensated, protected, and empowered against unfair treatment. And with their vast memberships, they wield tremendous power and influence as both a lobby and a potential voting bloc (Swain & Redding, 2019). Organized teachers deserve not a weakened, splintered, or disenfranchised union but rather one that refocuses its mission toward what is best for America's students in all schools.

Before educators or policy makers make any decision, and before activists form any opinion, they must always ask the question, "Is this good for students?" That is the direction that we must always follow, to which all other considerations are secondary. When charter school advocates lobby for less oversight, is it good for students? When anti–charter school voices call for wide-ranging charter moratoriums and fight against the closing of ineffective schools, is it good for students? When teachers' unions threaten to strike against firing ineffective educators, is it good for students? When politicians fight against fair funding formulas, is it good for students? What is best for students should take precedence; to do otherwise is unjust and has no place in our schools.

The largest teachers' union in the country, the NEA (2020), which has more than three million members, included in its policy statements for 2020–2021 the worthwhile platforms shared in table 4.1. I've outlined the reasons I support these policy platforms.

Table 4.1: The NEA's Worthwhile 2020–2021 Policy Platforms

Policy Platform	Reason to Support
The NEA (2020) reaffirms "its strong support for the use of affirmative action [the effort to improve opportunities for groups subjected to discrimination] in employment . . . to cure the effects of past ethnic or gender discrimination . . . and to achieve or maintain ethnic or gender diversity" (p. 4).	This policy acknowledges America's racist history and commits the nation's largest teachers' union to taking tangible steps toward diversifying the teacher workforce. For this, the NEA is to be commended.
The NEA (2020) believes that "all states should offer a publicly-funded, free, quality kindergarten program" (p. 10).	Long overdue, this commitment to universal kindergarten is necessary for a well-educated population and is unequivocally what is best for students.
The NEA (2020) believes that "educational programs and strategies designed to close the achievement and digital gaps must address equity issues related to broadband internet access" (p. 19).	It is necessary that all students have unfettered access to high-speed internet in order to learn and build the skills needed for the 21st century (Horn, 2020).
The NEA (2020) and its members are "committed to changing the policies and practices of the schools in which [they] work to end the school-to-prison pipeline" (p. 24).	The wide disciplinary disparities by race and ability have no place in schools committed to justice.

However, the NEA also put in its policy platforms the language in table 4.2, which I critique.

Table 4.2: The NEA's Misguided 2020–2021 Policy Platforms

Policy Platform	Criticism
The NEA (2020) opposes "the failed experiment of largely unaccountable privately managed charter schools while clarifying NEA's continued support for those public charter schools that are authorized and held accountable by local democratically elected school boards" (p. 27).	While this policy platform sounds reasonable, it is less so when looking at NEA chapters' calls for widespread blanket charter moratoriums. These moratoriums do not simply call for ending the expansion of so-called unaccountable charter schools; they call for a total cease of charter school expansion. This is akin to a monopoly preventing the development of competition. The bottom line is that if parents, predominantly in cities, did not want charter schools, then they would choose their local public school.
The NEA (2020) "opposes private school tuition voucher programs that pay for students to attend private schools *in order to obtain educational services that are available to them in public schools to which they have reasonable access*" (p. 7).	This policy platform is little more than turf warfare and a coveting of funding dollars. The union, essentially, is positioning itself against families that lack the financial means to enroll their children in private schools. It would therefore be interesting to see how many teachers' union members and teachers' union leaders choose to enroll their own children in private school. If any NEA union member or leader does so, this policy platform essentially denies less privileged families the very same privileged choices of union members and leaders.

These policies are not what is best for students, nor are they best for teachers. They are what is best for teachers' unions. These policies are precisely what is standing in the way of creating true nationwide coalitions that could dismantle America's broken education system.

Table 4.3 outlines platforms that I think the NEA *should* add to its policy statements. It is incumbent on union members to advocate for these proposed policies either through their individual building representatives or through local chapter elections.

Table 4.3: Platforms the NEA Should Add to Its Policy

Proposed Policy Platform	Support
A constitutional amendment guaranteeing the right to a quality education	It is unacceptable that the U.S. federal government does not guarantee a right to a quality education. By solely relying on state governments to ensure this basic human right, America's education system is stratified, unequal, inequitable, and unjust. A constitutional amendment would simultaneously raise the bar on what is acceptable in terms of quality education in the country and also signal that America truly values the education of its young people.
Fair funding formulas (revised using the methods described in table 2.1, page 39) in all fifty states	Teachers' union members teach in all schools, from the wealthiest and most highly resourced districts to the most impoverished and under-resourced. Any silence from a teachers' union in the face of the inequitable funding formulas that rig America's education system is complicity. Teachers' unions must wield their considerable power to ensure fair funding formulas.
An agreement on performance pay metrics and ineffective teacher termination in exchange for a baseline salary of $60,000 and a waiver of all student debt	Teachers' unions have been staunchly anti–performance pay for many years and have been equally assertive in the demands for higher pay. There is a deal to be made here, and it is one that would benefit students. Few industries in America ignore performance in their pay scales. Whether it is by commission, tips, bonuses, or pay raises, workers with higher production are rewarded and incentivized by increased pay. Teaching should be no different. While there are details to discuss on the intricacies of the performance pay scale, a starting point of $60,000, which could then rise based on a multifaceted formula involving teacher options, student surveys, and academic achievement, can incentivize teachers to become ever more effective. Ineffective teachers who remain ineffective after receiving supports should no longer be allowed to teach students. To further sweeten the deal, all teachers can have their student debt erased after three years of service.

Teachers who seek to change the direction of their unions face an uphill battle, but it is a battle worth fighting—and that is being fought. In Philadelphia, traditional public school teachers are represented by the Philadelphia Federation of Teachers (PFT). However, since 2019, a subset of teachers in the PFT have created a coalition of their own called Working Educators for a Stronger Union (WE; www.workingeducators .org) to push the PFT in different, often more pro-student and pro-family directions and challenging old-guard leadership union elections. While WE has problematic issues in their policies, the organization shows that challenging and changing union trajectories is possible.

Cease Fighting School Choice

School choice is a divisive term in American education. For some, school choice means parents deciding how and where to educate their children, be it homeschooling, traditional public, public charter, private with voucher, parochial, online, or any other form of school option. For others, school choice means diverting badly needed financial resources away from traditional public schools to other, potentially less effective options or privatizing options like public charter schools and private schools using vouchers. The following case study, however, offers a different way of understanding school choice.

Consider the following scenarios.

- **Family A's scenario:** Two parents are considering where to send their firstborn child to kindergarten. They are not thrilled with the local neighborhood public school. They are privileged with the financial means to afford private school tuition. They apply for a spot at the private school, and their child is admitted. They choose to enroll their child in the private school.

- **Family B's scenario:** Two parents are considering where to send their firstborn child to kindergarten. They are not thrilled with the local neighborhood public school. They would like to enroll their child in a school district in a neighboring town. Real estate costs more there, but they have the financial means to afford the necessary payments. They choose to move and enroll their child in their preferred neighborhood public school.

- **Family C's scenario:** Two parents are considering where to send their firstborn child to kindergarten. They are not thrilled with the local neighborhood public school. They cannot afford private school tuition. They cannot afford to move to a new town or district. They have no choice but to enroll their child in their local neighborhood public school and hope for the best.

- **Family D's scenario:** Two parents are considering where to send their firstborn child to kindergarten. They are not thrilled with the local neighborhood public school. They cannot afford private school tuition. They cannot afford to move to a new town, catchment, county, or district. They look around for options. In addition to their local neighborhood public school, there are a parochial school, a charter school, and a public magnet school. They consider a voucher for the parochial school. They consider applying to the public charter school lottery. They consider applying to the public magnet school. They decide to apply for all of them. They receive the results, then choose to enroll their child in the school that is best for their family.

Family A can still choose to pay private school tuition. Family B can still choose to move. Family C, however, has inequitable access to quality education based on the family's financial standing. But no longer is family D left without an option because it cannot afford one. This is the heart of school choice—ensuring all families have access to quality educational opportunities for their children, regardless of race, sexual orientation, gender expression, religion, socioeconomic status, or zip code.

Mobilize Parents and Families

Family is usually a child's greatest advocate, but often this advocacy is lost in the mires of educational jargon and bureaucracy, leaving families feeling isolated and powerless. This is where the National Parents Union (NPU; https://nationalparentsunion.org) comes in. The NPU amplifies parents' and caregivers' voices all across the country—particularly parents in traditionally marginalized communities: parents of color, parents who have low incomes, parents who have special needs, single parents, parents who have been incarcerated, and parents recovering from addiction.

With membership open to all, NPU's growing coalition supports and empowers parents as they agitate in their local communities for equitable and just educational opportunities for their children. An entire legislative division is focused on ensuring all states either live up to their state constitutional mandates of providing quality education for all children or advocating for state constitutional amendments to guarantee educational access. Downloadable tool kits (https://nationalparentsunion.org/parent-toolkit) help parents though the stages of advocacy, including organizing rallies and social media campaigns, connecting with school leaders and elected officials, and reaching out to local press and media.

 Lighthouse Beacon: *Tanesha Peeples and Hope + Outrage*

> Having grown up in Chicago, a city heavily motivated and dominated by politics that often fails to put students and families first, Tanesha Peeples is extremely critical of the delivery and quality of public education. In our conversations, she says it's imperative that activists understand the root causes and systemic barriers that prevent historically disenfranchised groups from accessing a quality education and teachers from getting the support they need to effectively serve families (T. Peeples, personal communication, May 6, 2020).

Peeples is deputy director of activist development for brightbeam and writes the blog *Hope + Outrage* (https://educationpost.org/tag/hope-and-outrage). She has practiced attacking the injustices created by the American education system *and* the gatekeepers to those systems by driving messaging that unifies those in the battle to dismantle those systems, all the while understanding the nuances that complicate the issues jeopardizing families' rights to quality education.

To Peeples, there are bad teachers and good teachers. Unfortunately, bad teachers' jobs are protected by unions. But without those unions, good teachers would not have certain protections such as health care and due process. There are administrators working to amplify the voices of marginalized communities and are genuinely advocating for them, while other decision makers are unwilling to even let them into the room. There are parents who actively engage in their kids' education and some who can certainly do better. Peeples understands these nuances, respects them, and refuses to adhere to the broad-stroke politics that so often poison the well of public discourse.

When it comes to navigating tensions between stakeholders, Peeples finds strength in sticking to public service and not politics. She advocates for the underserved and against opportunities and access only afforded to the privileged. Specifically, she pushed for the development of the Black Student Achievement Task Force. Its role was to advise and collaborate with Chicago Public Schools in policies, practices, and investments that support Black student achievement. She was successful in that push and is working on a plan to execute effective outreach and engagement to target families to identity needs and gaps, a plan modeled after a reparations plan the Los Angeles Unified School District developed.

In addition, Peeples mobilized communities in northern Illinois to advocate for the opening of high-quality schools in failing districts. She interviewed and hired a team of people in each community that conducted outreach to parents, specifically targeting demographics that the schools would serve. In Waukegan and North Chicago, she was able to collect over one thousand signatures supporting the opening of these charter schools, hold house meetings about what quality education looks like and how these new schools would deliver it, and finally mobilize a group of parents to speak at board approval hearings. After both communities denied the applications for the charter schools, Peeples and her coalition took the case to the Illinois State Board of Education's charter school commission and were able to get one of the applications approved.

When troubled, Peeples remembers the Honorable John Lewis, who famously got into "good trouble," and pledges to carry on that legacy by being brave enough to hold everyone accountable and challenge and dismantle systems of oppression.

Reflection Questions

Now that you have read this chapter, please consider the following questions. After reflecting alone, and then reflecting with a team if you are doing a book study, consider what actions you can take today. Who can you contact? What information can you research? Whose voice needs to be heard? What work needs to be done, and how can you be a part of it?

- When family members are choosing a school for a child, what types of options should they have?

- Is choosing to send a child to a private, parochial, or charter school equivalent to being "against" public education? How so? How not?

- Is exercising the privilege to purchase a home in a desirable school zone the same as exercising the privilege to send a child to a private, parochial, or charter school? How so? How not?

- Is a teachers' union supporting and protecting teachers the same as a teachers' union fighting for students? How so? How not?

- Imagine a fully resourced school empowered with everything it needs to support its students. What does that school look like? What does it not look like? What would it take to have such a school in every neighborhood or area across the country?

Epilogue

I remember my years at the University of Vermont in the early 2000s as days of idealism, filled with passionate peers who were driven with enthusiastic resolve to change the world around them. People who created alternative fuel vehicles to travel across the country, devoted themselves to sustainable organic farming, pushed boundaries through international travel, created music, made art, and started businesses that prioritized people over profits.

These were types of people I hadn't met before—people who saw the world through a prism of kindness, happiness, and justice rather than one of salaries, rankings, and reputations. These people saw the world as ripe for change. I couldn't help but learn from these people. Many years later, I have devoted myself to a philosophy of hyperlocal activism—to the ripples I can make in my little corner of the world, which can resonate outward.

So often, those of us who work for justice and equity look outward. We look to other communities to serve; we see the inequitable school funding formulas, the racism, the political squabbling. They're enough to make us weep and sink into paralyzed apathy. After all, the injustices are so great, the issues so large, what can one person do? What ripples can one stone make in a sea so vast?

This is where commitment to hyperlocal activism comes in. No single person can change the world; no single person can dismantle America's broken system of education. But every individual has a locus of control, a stone to throw, and an ability to agitate, inform, and change a community. Working for justice is about our babies—all our babies. It's about living up to the morality of our words. It's another small stone, a tiny ripple in the sea. When I think back on those passionate people who taught me so much, I think of the ripples we can all make and the pebbles we can all throw. And I begin to see the tidal wave of positive change in education that we can inspire by taking action in our little corners of the country—all of us making our vital contributions to dismantling the broken system of American education.

Appendix
Suggested Resources and Readings

As activists and educators, our learning must continue. But often, with so much to read and learn in so little time, it is hard to know where to begin. Here are some places to start.

Books

- *The Body Keeps the Score: Brain, Mind, and Body in the Healing of Trauma* by Bessel van der Kolk (2014)

- *Case Studies on Diversity and Social Justice Education* by Paul C. Gorski and Seema G. Pothini (2018)

- *Caste: The Origins of Our Discontents* by Isabel Wilkerson (2020)

- *The Color of Law: A Forgotten History of How Our Government Segregated America* by Richard Rothstein (2017)

- *Culturally Responsive Teaching and the Brain: Promoting Authentic Engagement and Rigor Among Culturally and Linguistically Diverse Students* by Zaretta Hammond (2015)

- *Financing Public Schools: Theory, Policy, and Practice* by Kern Alexander, Richard G. Salmon, and F. King Alexander (2015)

- *Other People's Children: Cultural Conflict in the Classroom* by Lisa Delpit (2006)

- *Pedagogy of the Oppressed* by Paulo Freire (2018)

- *A People's History of the United States* by Howard Zinn (2015)

- *Pushout: The Criminalization of Black Girls in School* by Monique W. Morris (2016)

- *Slavery's Capitalism: A New History of American Economic Development* edited by Sven Beckert and Seth Rockman (2016)

- *Stamped From the Beginning: The Definitive History of Racist Ideas in America* by Ibram X. Kendi (2016)

- *Teacher Education Around the World: Changing Policies and Practices* edited by Linda Darling-Hammond and Ann Lieberman (2012)

- *We Want to Do More Than Survive: Abolitionist Teaching and the Pursuit of Educational Freedom* by Bettina L. Love (2019)

- *The White Architects of Black Education: Ideology and Power in America, 1865–1954* by William H. Watkins (2001)

- *White Fragility: Why It's So Hard for White People to Talk About Racism* by Robin DiAngelo (2018)

Podcasts

- *#BuildingPower* at https://bit.ly/3bUdWqN

- *1619* at https://apple.co/30a9MbR and https://spoti.fi/3CZ7M4t

- *8 Black Hands* at https://anchor.fm/8-black-hands-podcast

- *Be Antiracist With Ibram X. Kendi* at www.ibramxkendi.com/be -antiracist-podcast

- *Nice White Parents* at https://apple.co/3kh4WAA

- *The Recess Podcast* at https://apple.co/3BXsbFE

- *Talk Dat Real Sh*t* at https://citizen.education/category/talk-dat-real-sht

- *Throughline* at www.npr.org/podcasts/510333/throughline

- *UnPublic With Citizen Stewart* at https://citizen.education/unpublic

Social Media

- The Black Wall Street Times at https://theblackwallsttimes.com

- We, the motherhood at https://wethemotherhood.com

References and Resources

The 74. (n.d.). *40% of America's public schools don't have a single educator of color. How the new nonprofit BranchED is looking to rethink that minority teacher pipeline.* Accessed at www.the74 million.org/article/40-percent-of-americas-public-schools-dont-have-a-single-educator-of-color -how-the-new-non-profit-branched-is-looking-to-rethink-that-minority-teacher-pipeline on October 13, 2021.

AFP. (2021). *$28 million: The cost of flying into space with the world's richest man Jeff Bezos.* Accessed at https://economictimes.indiatimes.com/news/science/28-million-the-cost-of-flying -into-space-with-the-worlds-richest-man-jeff-bezos/trip-to-space-with-jeff-bezos/slideshow /83478635.cms on October 12, 2021.

Alexander, K., Salmon, R. G., & Alexander, F. K. (2015). *Financing public schools: Theory, policy, and practice.* New York: Routledge.

Alexander, M. (2020). *The new Jim Crow: Mass incarceration in the age of colorblindness* (10th anniversary ed.). New York: The New Press.

Ali, D. (2018, July 12). *Effective use of letter writing campaigns and sample letter templates for #SAadvocates* [Blog post]. Accessed at www.naspa.org/blog/effective-use-of-letter-writing -campaigns-and-sample-letter-templates-for-saadvocates on October 12, 2021.

Baptist, E. E. (2016). Toward a political economy of slave labor: Hands, whipping-machines, and modern power. In S. Beckert & S. Rockman (Eds.), *Slavery's capitalism: A new history of American economic development* (pp. 31–61). Philadelphia: University of Pennsylvania Press.

APM Reports. (n.d.). *The FBI's war on King.* Accessed at https://features.apmreports.org/arw/king indent

Barnum, M. (2017). *Certification rules and tests are keeping would-be teachers of color out of America's classrooms. Here's how.* Accessed at www.chalkbeat.org/2017/9/12/21100902/certification-rules -and-tests-are-keeping-would-be-teachers-of-color-out-of-america-s-classrooms-her on October 12, 2021.

Beatty, P. (2015). *The sellout.* New York: Farrar, Straus & Giroux.

Beckert, S., & Rockman, S. (Eds.). (2016). *Slavery's capitalism: A new history of American economic development.* Philadelphia: University of Pennsylvania Press.

Belser, C. T., Shillingford, M. A., & Joe, J. R. (2016). The ASCA model and a multi-tiered system of supports: A framework to support students of color with problem behavior. *The Professional Counselor, 6*(3), 251–262.

Beracha, E., & Hardin, W. G., III. (2018). The capitalization of school quality into renter and owner housing. *Real Estate Economics, 46*(1), 85–119.

Bergeron, B. S. (2008). Enacting a culturally responsive curriculum in a novice teacher's classroom: Encountering disequilibrium. *Urban Education, 43*(1), 4–28.

Bishop, R. S. (1990). Mirrors, windows, and sliding glass doors. *Perspectives, 6*(3), ix–xi.

Bogin, A., & Nguyen-Hoang, P. (2014). Property left behind: An unintended consequence of a No Child Left Behind "failing" school designation. *Journal of Regional Science, 54*(5), 788–805.

Bolger, M. (n.d.). *Social justice toolbox: Privilege for sale.* Accessed at www.socialjusticetoolbox.com /activity/privilege-for-sale on March 30, 2021.

Boodry, K. (2016). August Belmont and the world the slaves made. In S. Beckert & S. Rockman (Eds.), *Slavery's capitalism: A new history of American economic development* (pp. 163–178). Philadelphia: University of Pennsylvania Press.

Bordewich, F. M. (1996). *Killing the White man's Indian: Reinventing of Native Americans at the end of the twentieth century.* New York: Doubleday.

Brown, D. (1970). *Bury my heart at Wounded Knee: An Indian history of the American West.* New York: Holt, Rinehart & Winston.

Brown v. Board of Education of Topeka, 347 U.S. 483 (1954).

Brubaker, H. (2020). *Students protest education inequity in march from Lower Merion to Philly's Overbrook High School.* Accessed at www.inquirer.com/news/lower-merion-overbrook-protest -inequity-schools-i-will-breathe-20200830.html on October 12, 2021.

Buffum, A., Mattos, M., & Malone, J. (2018). *Taking action: A handbook for RTI at Work.* Bloomington, IN: Solution Tree Press.

Cabrera, N. L., Milem, J. F., Jaquette, O., & Marx, R. W. (2014). Missing the (student achievement) forest for all the (political) trees: Empiricism and the Mexican American studies controversy in Tucson. *American Education Research Journal, 51*(6), 1084–1118.

Camera, L. (2019). *International survey: U.S. teachers are overworked, feel underappreciated.* Accessed at www.usnews.com/news/education-news/articles/2019-06-19/international-survey-us-teachers -are-overworked-feel-underappreciated on October 12, 2021.

Campanile, C. (2015). *Teachers union contributed $4.7M to political activities last year.* Accessed at https://nypost.com/2015/01/19/teachers-union-contributed-4-7m-to-political-activities-last-year on October 13, 2021.

Carlin, G., Hamza, J., Mangone, R. J., Rickabaugh, K. (Producers), & Urbisci, R. (Producer & Director). (2005). George Carlin: *Life is worth losing* [Television special]. United States: Cable Stuff Productions.

Carothers, D., Aydin, H., & Houdyshell, M. (2019). Teacher shortages and cultural mismatch: District and university collaboration for recruiting. *Journal of Social Studies Education Research, 10*(3) 39–63.

Carver-Thomas, D. (2018, April). *Diversifying the teaching profession: How to recruit and retain teachers of color*. Palo Alto, CA: Learning Policy Institute.

Center for Black Educator Development. (n.d.). *About us*. Accessed at www.thecenterblacked.org /about-us on July 9, 2021.

The Century Foundation. (2019). *The benefits of socioeconomically and racially integrated schools and classrooms*. Accessed at https://tcf.org/content/facts/the-benefits-of-socioeconomically-and-racially -integrated-schools-and-classrooms on October 12, 2021.

Children's Defense Fund. (2021). *The state of America's children: 2021*. Accessed at www.childrens defense.org/wp-content/uploads/2021/04/The-State-of-Americas-Children-2021.pdf on October 11, 2021.

Clear, J. (n.d.). *The beginner's guide to deliberate practice*. Accessed at https://jamesclear.com/beginners -guide-deliberate-practice on October 13, 2021.

Cochran-Smith, M., Carney, M. C., Keefe, E. S., Burton, S., Chang, W.-C., Fernández, M. B., et al. (2018). *Reclaiming accountability in teacher education*. New York: Teachers College Press.

Conlin, M., & Jalilevand, M. (2015). *Systemic inequities in special education financing*. Accessed at www.jstor.org/stable/24459301 on October 11, 2021.

Coulson, A. J. (2010). The effects of teachers unions on American education. *Cato Journal*, *30*(1), 155–170.

Coval, K., Lansana, Q. A., & Marshall, N. (Eds.). (2015). *The BreakBeat Poets: New American poetry in the age of hip-hop*. Chicago: Haymarket Books.

Cummings, M. (2018). *Study shows newspaper op-eds change minds*. Accessed at https://news.yale.edu /2018/04/24/study-shows-newspaper-op-eds-change-minds on October 12, 2021.

Darling-Hammond, L., & Lieberman, A. (Eds.). (2012). *Teacher education around the world: Changing policies and practices*. New York: Routledge.

Dee, T., & Penner, E. (2016). *The causal effects of cultural relevance: Evidence from an ethnic studies curriculum*. Accessed at https://cepa.stanford.edu/sites/default/files/wp16-01-v201601.pdf on October 28, 2021.

Dee, T., & Penner, E. (2019). *My brother's keeper? The impact of targeted educational supports*. Accessed at https://cepa.stanford.edu/sites/default/files/wp19-07-v201910.pdf on October 28, 2021.

de la Horra, L. P. (2017, July 15). *The Southern slave economy was anti-capitalistic*. Accessed at https://fee.org/articles/the-southern-slave-economy-was-anti-capitalistic on June 23, 2021.

Delpit, L. (2006). *Other people's children: Cultural conflict in the classroom*. New York: The New Press.

DiAngelo, R. (2018). *White fragility: Why it's so hard for White people to talk about racism*. Boston: Beacon Press.

Dougherty, J., Harrelson, J., Maloney, L., Murphy, D., Smith, R., Snow, M., et al. (2009). School choice in suburbia: Test scores, race, and housing markets. *American Journal of Education*, *115*(4), 523–548.

Douglass, F. (1857). "West India emancipation" [Speech]. Accessed at www.blackpast.org/african -american-history/1857-frederick-douglass-if-there-no-struggle-there-no-progress on October 11, 2021.

Douglass, F. (2002). *Narrative of the life of Frederick Douglass: An American slave, written by himself.* London: Collins. (Original work published 1845)

Dray, P. (2003). *At the hands of persons unknown: The lynching of Black America.* New York: The Modern Library.

Duncombe, W. D., & Yinger, J. (2004). *How much more does a disadvantaged student cost?* Accessed at https://surface.syr.edu/cgi/viewcontent.cgi?article=1102&context=cpr on October 12, 2021.

Education Law Center. (n.d.). *State profiles: California.* Accessed at https://edlawcenter.org/litigation /states/california.html on March 31, 2021.

Education Trust. (n.d.). *Is your state prioritizing teacher diversity and equity?* Accessed at https://edtrust.org/educator-diversity/#US on June 23, 2021.

Education Trust. (2020). *Black and Latino students shut out of advanced coursework opportunities.* Accessed at https://edtrust.org/press-release/black-and-latino-students-shut-out-of-advanced -coursework-opportunities on October 10, 2021.

ETS. (n.d.a). *About the* Praxis *tests.* Accessed at www.ets.org/praxis/institutions/about on October 12, 2021.

ETS. (n.d.b). *Test and service fees.* Accessed at www.ets.org/praxis/register/fees on October 13, 2021.

Every Student Succeeds Act of 2015, Pub. L. No. 114-95, 20 U.S.C. § 1177 (2015).

Flanagan, C. (2021). *Private schools have become truly obscene.* Accessed at www.theatlantic.com /magazine/archive/2021/04/private-schools-are-indefensible/618078 on October 12, 2021.

Freire, P. (2018). *Pedagogy of the oppressed* (50th anniversary ed.). New York: Bloomsbury.

Gay, G. (2018). *Culturally responsive teaching: Theory, research, and practice* (3rd ed.). New York: Teachers College Press.

Goings, R. B., & Bianco, M. (2016). It's hard to be who you don't see: An exploration of Black male high school students' perspectives on becoming teachers. *Urban Review, 48*(4), 628–646.

Goldberg, B., & Shubinski, B. (2020). *Black education and Rockefeller philanthropy from the Jim Crow south to the civil rights era.* Accessed at https://resource.rockarch.org/story/black -education-and-rockefeller-philanthropy-from-the-jim-crow-south-to-the-civil-rights-era on October 25, 2021.

Goldstein, A., & Hastings, O. P. (2019). Buying in: Positional competition, schools, income inequality, and housing consumption. *Sociological Science, 6*(16), 416–445.

Goode, R. W. (2017). *Charter schools thrive under strict oversight.* Accessed at www.blackenterprise .com/charter-schools-thrive-strict-oversight/?test=prebid on October 13, 2021.

Goodell, W. (1853). *The American slave code in theory and practice: Its distinctive features shown by its statutes, judicial decisions, and illustrative facts.* New York: American and Foreign Anti-Slavery Society.

Gorski, P. C. (n.d.). *Stages of multicultural curriculum transformation.* Accessed at www.edchange.org /multicultural/curriculum/steps.html on October 10, 2021.

Gorski, P. C. (2016). Poverty and the ideological imperative: A call to unhook from deficit and grit ideology and to strive for structural ideology in teacher education. *Journal of Education for Teaching, 42*(4), 378–386.

Gorski, P. C., & Pothini, S. G. (2018). *Case studies on diversity and social justice education* (2nd ed.). New York: Routledge.

Hammond, Z. (2015). *Culturally responsive teaching and the brain: Promoting authentic engagement and rigor among culturally and linguistically diverse students.* Thousand Oaks, CA: Corwin Press.

Hanford, E. (2018, September 10). *Hard words: Why aren't kids being taught to read?* Accessed at www.apmreports.org/episode/2018/09/10/hard-words-why-american-kids-arent-being-taught-to-read on March 31, 2021.

Hanna, M. (2020). *Wolf pushing charter-school bill that would change funding, accountability rules.* Accessed at www.inquirer.com/news/charter-school-reform-pennsylvania-tom-wolf-budget-2020 0203.html on October 13, 2021.

Hannah-Jones, N. (2019, August 14). *The 1619 project.* Accessed at www.nytimes.com/interactive /2019/08/14/magazine/1619-america-slavery.html on March 31, 2021.

Hansen, M., & Quintero, D. (2018). *School leadership: An untapped opportunity to draw young people of color into teaching.* Accessed at www.brookings.edu/blog/brown-center-chalkboard/2018/11/26 /school-leadership-an-untapped-opportunity-to-draw-young-people-of-color-into-teaching on October 13, 2021.

Henry, G. T., Campbell, S. L., Thompson, C. L., Patriarca, L. A., Luterbach, K. J., Lys, D. B., et al. (2013). The predictive validity of measures of teacher candidate programs and performance: Toward an evidence-based approach to teacher preparation. *Journal of Teacher Education, 64*(5), 439–453.

Hester, O. R., Bridges, S. A., & Rollins, L. H. (2020). "Overworked and underappreciated": Special education teachers describe stress and attrition. *Teacher Development, 24*(3), 348–365.

Hill, K. K. (2016). *Beyond the rope: The impact of lynching on black culture and memory.* Cambridge, England: Cambridge University Press.

hooks, b. (1995). *Killing rage: Ending racism.* New York: Holt.

Horn, M. B. (2020). *How to get every student a device and access to the internet.* Accessed at www.forbes.com/sites/michaelhorn/2020/06/18/how-to-get-every-student-a-device-and-access-to -the-internet/?sh=75f999bc15c9 on October 13, 2021.

Houston, J. W., & Houston, J. D. (1973). *Farewell to Manzanar.* Boston: Houghton Mifflin.

Howard, J. (2018). The white kid can do whatever he wants: The racial socialization of a gifted education program. *Educational Studies, 54*(5), 553–568.

Hyman, J. (2017). Does money matter in the long run? Effects of school spending on educational attainment. *American Economic Journal: Economic Policy, 9*(4), 256–280.

Iasevoli, B. (2018, August 3). New teachers are often assigned to high-poverty schools. Why not train them there? *Education Week.* Accessed at www.edweek.org/leadership/new-teachers-are-often -assigned-to-high-poverty-schools-why-not-train-them-there/2018/08 on March 31, 2021.

Jackson, C. K., Johnson, R. C., & Persico, C. (2016). The effects of school spending on educational and economic outcomes: Evidence from school finance reforms. *Quarterly Journal of Economics, 131*(1), 157–218.

Jarecki, E. (Producer & Director), & Shopsin, M. (Producer). (2012). *The house I live in* [Video file]. United States: Abramorama.

Jiminez, L., Sargrad, S., Morales, J., & Thompson, M. (2016). *Remedial education.* Accessed at www.americanprogress.org/issues/education-k-12/reports/2016/09/28/144000/remedial-education on October 12, 2021.

Jones, F. H., Jones, P., & Jones, J. L. (2007). *Tools for teaching: Discipline, instruction, motivation.* Santa Cruz, CA: Authors.

Kendi, I. X. (2016). *Stamped from the beginning: The definitive history of racist ideas in America.* New York: Bold Type Books.

Kendi, I. X. (2019). *How to be an antiracist.* New York: One World.

Kimball, E. (2016). "What have we to do with slavery?" New Englanders and the slave economies of the West Indies. In S. Beckert & S. Rockman (Eds.), *Slavery's capitalism: A new history of American economic development* (pp. 181–194). Philadelphia: University of Pennsylvania Press.

King, M. L., Jr. (2010). "I Have a Dream" speech, in its entirety [Speech transcript]. *NPR.* Accessed at www.npr.org/2010/01/18/122701268/i-have-a-dream-speech-in-its-entirety on July 21, 2021. (Original work published 1963)

Ladson-Billings, G. (2004). Landing on the wrong note: The price we paid for *Brown. Educational Researcher, 33*(7), 3–13.

Laukaitis, J. (2017). Ravitch reversed: Ideology and the history of American education reform. *American Educational History Journal, 44*(1), 21–31.

Lemov, D. (2015). *Teach like a champion 2.0: 62 techniques that put students on the path to college* (2nd ed.). Hoboken, NJ: Wiley.

Leonard, F. [@franklinleonard]. (2015, October 10). *When you're accustomed to privilege, equality feels like oppression. (It's not.)* [Tweet]. Twitter. Accessed at https://twitter.com/franklinleonard/status/652885246220734464?lang=en%202015 on October 12, 2021.

Levin, J., de los Reyes, I. B., Atchison, D., Manship, K., Arellanes, M., & Hu, L. (2018). *What does it cost to educate California's students? A professional judgement approach report appendices.* Accessed at https://files.eric.ed.gov/fulltext/ED594741.pdf on October 28, 2021.

Loewenberg, D. (2018, July 6). *Teacher residencies: The future of teacher prep?* [Blog post]. Accessed at www.ewa.org/blog-educated-reporter/teacher-residencies-future-teacher-prep on March 31, 2021.

Logan, J. R., Weiwei Z., & Oakley, D. (2017). Court orders, white flight, and school district segregation. *Social Forces, 95*(3), 1049–1075.

Loh, T. H., Coes, C., & Buthe, B. (2020). *The great real estate reset.* Accessed at www.brookings.edu/essay/trend-1-separate-and-unequal-neighborhoods-are-sustaining-racial-and-economic-injustice-in-the-us on October 12, 2021.

Love, B. L. (2019). *We want to do more than survive: Abolitionist teaching and the pursuit of educational freedom.* Boston: Beacon Press.

Lutz, M. (2017). *The hidden cost of* Brown v. Board: *African American educators' resistance to desegregating schools.* Accessed at https://newprairiepress.org/ojrrp/vol12/iss4/2 on October 12, 2021.

Mahoney, M. H. (2013). Inequity in American schools: A new perspective on the distributional effects of school expenditures on economic well-being. *Review of Income and Wealth, 59*(4), 728–755.

Malcolm X. (1965a). *The autobiography of Malcolm X.* New York: Grove Press.

Malcolm X. (1965b). "With Mrs. Fannie Lou Hamer" [Speech]. In G. Breitman (Ed.) *Malcolm X speaks: Selected speeches and statements.* New York: Grove Press.

McDaniels, A. (2017, December 19). *A new path for school integration.* Accessed at www.american progress.org/issues/education-k-12/news/2017/12/19/444212/new-path-school-integration on March 31, 2021.

Milner, H. R., & Howard, T. C. (2004). Black teachers, Black students, Black communities, and *Brown*: Perspectives and insights from experts. *The Journal of Negro Education, 73*(3), 285–297.

Montessori, M. (1995). *The absorbent mind: A classic in education and child development for educators and parents.* New York: Holt.

Mordechay, K. (n.d.). *The demographics of America's schools are changing, and policymakers need to be up to the challenge* [Blog post]. Accessed at https://blogs.lse.ac.uk/usappblog/2017/11/01 /the-demographics-of-americas-schools-are-changing-and-policymakers-need-to-be-up-to-the -challenge on November 8, 2021.

Morgan, I., & Amerikaner, A. (2018, February 27). *Funding gaps 2018: An analysis of school funding equity across the U.S. and within each state.* Washington, DC: The Education Trust.

Morris, M. W. (2016). *Pushout: The criminalization of Black girls in school.* New York: The New Press.

Morrison, T. (1987). *Beloved.* New York: Knopf.

Morsy, L., & Rothstein, R. (2019). *Toxic stress and children's outcomes.* Accessed at www.epi.org /publication/toxic-stress-and-childrens-outcomes-african-american-children-growing-up-poor-are -at-greater-risk-of-disrupted-physiological-functioning-and-depressed-academic-achievement on October 11, 2021.

NAACP Legal Defense and Educational Fund. (n.d.). Brown v. Board of Education: *Celebrating the 67th anniversary of LDF's seminal case.* Accessed at www.naacpldf.org/brown-vs-board on June 23, 2021.

National Association for College Admission Counseling & American School Counselor Association. (n.d.). *State-by-state student-to-counselor ratio report: 10-year trends.* Accessed at www.nacacnet.org /globalassets/documents/publications/research/state-by-state-ratio-report.pdf on October 11, 2021.

National Center for Education Statistics. (n.d.a). *Characteristics of public school teachers.* Accessed at https://nces.ed.gov/programs/coe/indicator/clr on October 25, 2021.

National Center for Education Statistics. (n.d.b). *Common Core of Data district locator.* Accessed at https://nces.ed.gov/ccd/districtsearch on June 23, 2021.

National Center for Education Statistics. (n.d.c). *Expenditures.* Accessed at https://nces.ed.gov/fast facts/display.asp?id=66 on October 13, 2021.

National Center for Education Statistics. (n.d.d). *Public school district finance peer search.* Accessed at https://nces.ed.gov/edfin/search/search_intro.asp on June 23, 2021.

National Center for Education Statistics. (2021a). *Racial/ethnic enrollment in public schools.* Accessed at https://nces.ed.gov/programs/coe/indicator_cge.asp on July 1, 2021.

National Center for Education Statistics. (2021b). *Status dropout rates.* Accessed at https://nces.ed .gov/programs/coe/indicator/coj on October 10, 2021.

National Center for Teacher Residencies. (n.d.). *Impact and results.* Accessed at https://nctresidencies .org/about/impact-results on March 31, 2021.

National Education Association. (n.d.a). *Charter school accountability.* Accessed at www.nea.org /student-success/smart-just-policies/funding-public-schools/charter-school-accountability on October 13, 2021.

National Education Association. (n.d.b). *Opposing vouchers.* Accessed at www.nea.org/student -success/smart-just-policies/funding-public-schools/opposing-vouchers on October 13, 2021.

National Education Association. (2020). *National Education Association policy statements 2020–2021.* Accessed at www.nea.org/sites/default/files/2020-09/NEA%20Policy%20Statements%202020-21.pdf on March 31, 2021.

National Park Service. (2015). *The Hampton model.* Accessed at www.nps.gov/bowa/learn/history culture/the-hampton-model.htm on October 8, 2021.

Newsom, J. S. (Producer & Director), & Costanzo, J. (Producer). (2011). *Miss representation* [Film]. United States: Girls' Club Entertainment.

OpenSecrets. (n.d.). *Teachers unions.* Accessed at www.opensecrets.org/industries/indus.php?ind=l1 300 on October 13, 2021.

Osborn, D. (2018). *The words "we" use for "the other."* Accessed at www.learningforjustice.org /magazine/the-words-we-use-for-the-other on October 10, 2021.

Papageorge, N. W., Gershenson, S., & Kang, K. M. (2020). Teacher expectations matter. *The Review of Economics and Statistics, 102*(2), 234–251.

Partelow, L., Spong, A., Brown, C., & Johnson, S. (2017, September 14). *America needs more teachers of color and a more selective teaching profession.* Accessed at www.americanprogress.org /issues/education-k-12/reports/2017/09/14/437667/america-needs-teachers-color-selective -teaching-profession on March 31, 2021.

PayScale. (n.d.). *Average salary for the School District of Philadelphia employees.* Accessed at www.pay scale.com/research/US/Employer=The_School_District_of_Philadelphia/Salary on October 12, 2021.

Pennsylvania Department of Education. (n.d.). *Future ready PA index.* Accessed at https://future readypa.org/# on November 30, 2021.

Petchauer, E. (2012). Teacher licensure exams and Black teacher candidates: Toward new theory and promising practice. *The Journal of Negro Education, 81*(3), 252–267.

Peter G. Peterson Foundation. (2021). *Budget basics: National defense.* Accessed at www.pgpf.org /budget-basics/budget-explainer-national-defense on October 12, 2021.

Peters, A. L. (2019). Desegregation and the (dis)integration of Black school leaders: Reflections on the impact of *Brown v. Board of Education* on Black education. *Peabody Journal of Education, 94*(5), 521–534.

Petry, A. (1946). *The street.* Boston: Houghton Mifflin.

Piaget, J., & Inhelder, B. (1969). *The psychology of the child.* Paris, France: Basic Books.

Plessy v. Ferguson, 163 U.S. 537 (1896).

Pouncey, W. C., Ennis, L. S., Woolley, T. W., & Connell, P. H. (2013). School funding issues: State legislators and school superintendents—Adversaries or allies? *SAGE Open, 3*(2), 1–13.

Quinton, S., & National Journal. (2014). *The race gap in high school honors classes.* Accessed at www.theatlantic.com/politics/archive/2014/12/the-race-gap-in-high-school-honors-classes /431751 on October 25, 2021.

Ringelstein, Z. (2018). *Save public education by raising teacher salaries to $60K federal minimum.* Accessed at www.forbes.com/sites/zakringelstein/2018/09/05/save-public-education-by-raising -teacher-salaries-to-60k-federal-minimum/?sh=42a7df0e7afa on October 13, 2021.

Rothstein, R. (2017). *The color of law: A forgotten history of how our government segregated America.* New York: Liveright.

Sattin-Bajaj, C., & Roda, A. (2020). Opportunity hoarding in school choice contexts: The role of policy design in promoting middle-class parents' exclusionary behaviors. *Educational Policy, 34*(7), 992–1035.

Schaap, H., & de Bruijn, E. (2018). Elements affecting the development of professional learning communities in schools. *Learning Environments Research, 21*(1), 109–134.

Seiki, S. (2019). Living restoration: Discipline over punishment—Successes and struggles with restorative justice in schools. *Multicultural Perspectives, 21*(3), 174–176.

Semuels, A. (2016). *Good school, rich school; bad school, poor school.* Accessed at www.theatlantic.com/business/archive/2016/08/property-taxes-and-unequal-schools/497333 on November 30, 2021.

Serrano v. Priest, 5 Cal.3d 584 (1971).

Serrano v. Priest, 18 Cal.3d 728 (1976).

Shapiro, E. (2021). *Only 8 black students are admitted to Stuyvesant High School.* Accessed at www.nytimes.com/2021/04/29/nyregion/stuyvestant-black-students.html on October 25, 2021.

Simon, S. (2013). *Special report: Class struggle—How charter schools get students they want.* Accessed at www.reuters.com/article/us-usa-charters-admissions/special-report-class-struggle-how-charter-schools-get-students-they-want-idUSBRE91E0HF20130215 on October 13, 2021.

Sister District Action Network. (2020). *Field research overview.* Accessed at https://sisterdistrict.com/wp-content/uploads/2020/01/Field-Research-Overview.pdf on October 12, 2021.

Skinner, B. F. (1947). "Superstition" in the pigeon. *Journal of Experimental Psychology, 38,* 168–172.

Sparks, S. D. (2020, February 25). *Hidden segregation within schools is tracked in new study.* Accessed at www.edweek.org/leadership/hidden-segregation-within-schools-is-tracked-in-new-study/2020/02 on March 31, 2021.

Stanford Encyclopedia of Philosophy. (2021). *Public goods.* Accessed at https://plato.stanford.edu/entries/public-goods on October 11, 2021.

Starecheski, L. (2015). *Take the ACE quiz—and learn what it does and doesn't mean.* Accessed at www.npr.org/sections/health-shots/2015/03/02/387007941/take-the-ace-quiz-and-learn-what-it-does-and-doesnt-mean on October 12, 2021.

Stevenson, B. (2019). *Just mercy: A story of justice and redemption.* New York: Spiegel & Grau.

Substance Abuse and Mental Health Services Administration. (2021). *Understanding child trauma.* Accessed at www.samhsa.gov/child-trauma/understanding-child-trauma on October 11, 2021.

Swain, W. A., & Redding, C. (2019). Teachers' union power in a budget crunch: Lasting ramifications of differential spending responses to the great recession. *Educational Policy.* https://doi: 10.1177/0895904819881161

Title VIII of the Civil Rights Act of 1968, 42 U.S.C. 3601-3619 (1968).

Trinacria, J. (2017). *Lower Merion teachers are highest paid in state, but they want more.* Accessed at www.phillymag.com/news/2017/09/05/lower-merion-teachers-petition-higher-wages on October 12, 2021.

Twain, M. (1884). *Adventures of Huckleberry Finn.* London: Chatto & Windus.

United Negro College Fund. (n.d.). *K–12 disparity facts and statistics.* Accessed at https://uncf.org/pages/k-12-disparity-facts-and-stats on October 13, 2021.

USAspending.gov. (n.d.). *In 2021, the government spent $6.82 trillion.* Accessed at https://datalab .usaspending.gov/americas-finance-guide/spending/#:~:text=In%20Fiscal%20Year%20 2021%2C%20federal,that%20year%20(%2422.39%20trillion) on October 28, 2021.

U.S. Bureau of Labor Statistics. (2013). *Apprenticeship: Earn while you learn.* Accessed at www.bls .gov/careeroutlook/2013/summer/art01.pdf on October 26, 2021.

U.S. Census Bureau. (2019). *American Community Survey 5-year estimates.* Accessed at https://censusreporter.org/profiles/86000US19131-19131 on October 6, 2021.

U.S. Department of Education Office for Civil Rights. (2014, March). *Civil Rights Data Collection: Data snapshot—School discipline* (Issue Brief No. 1). Accessed at https://ocrdata.ed.gov/assets /downloads/CRDC-School-Discipline-Snapshot.pdf on July 13, 2021.

van der Kolk, B. (2014). *The body keeps the score: Brain, mind, and body in the healing of trauma.* New York: Penguin.

Villegas, A. M., & Lucas, T. (2002). *Educating culturally responsive teachers: A coherent approach.* Albany: State University of New York Press.

Vygotsky, L. S. (1962). *Thought and language.* Cambridge, MA: MIT Press.

Walker, T. (2018). *"Education is political": Neutrality in the classroom shortchanges students.* Accessed at www.nea.org/advocating-for-change/new-from-nea/education-political-neutrality-classroom -shortchanges-students on November 30, 2021.

Walker, V. S. (2018). *The lost education of Horace Tate: Uncovering the hidden heroes who fought for justice in schools.* New York: The New Press.

Watkins, W. H. (2001). *The White architects of Black education: Ideology and power in America, 1865–1954.* New York: Teachers College Press.

Waxman, O. B. (2019). *The first Africans in Virginia landed in 1619. It was a turning point for slavery in American history—but not the beginning.* Accessed at https://time.com/5653369/august-1619 -jamestown-history on October 6, 2021.

Whitehead, C. (2016). *The underground railroad.* New York: Doubleday.

Whitford, D. K., Zhang, D., & Katsiyannis, A. (2018). Traditional vs. alternative teacher preparation programs: A meta-analysis. *Journal of Child and Family Studies, 27*(3), 671–685.

Wilkerson, I. (2010). *The warmth of other suns: The epic story of America's Great Migration.* New York: Vintage Books.

Wilkerson, I. (2020). *Caste: The origins of our discontents.* New York: Random House.

Wong, A. (2018, November 28). The students suing for a constitutional right to education. *The Atlantic.* Accessed at www.theatlantic.com/education/archive/2018/11/lawsuit-constitutional -right-education/576901 on July 5, 2021.

Wright, Z. (2018). *I can't spare my son his struggles, but I can be there when he triumphs.* Accessed at https://educationpost.org/i-cant-spare-my-son-his-struggles-but-i-can-be-there-when-he-triumphs on October 13, 2021.

Wright, Z. (2019). *There's a difference between a "good" school and choosing Whiteness and wealth.* Accessed at https://educationpost.org/theres-a-difference-between-a-good-school-and-choosing -whiteness-and-wealth on October 13, 2021.

Zinn, H. (2015). *A people's history of the United States.* New York: Harper Perennial.

Index